UNSTOPPABLE

Unstoppable

An Inspiring Story of an Israeli Actress

Sheena Ray Reynolds

©2025 All Rights Reserved. No portion of this book may be reproduced, stored in a retrieval system, or transmitted in any form or by any means—electronic, mechanical, photocopy, recording, scanning, or other—except for brief quotations in critical reviews or articles without the prior permission of the author.

Published by Game Changer Publishing

Paperback ISBN: 978-1-967424-96-2
Hardcover ISBN: 978-1-967424-97-9
Digital ISBN: 978-1-967424-98-6

www.GameChangerPublishing.com

This book is dedicated to the Universe and all the beautiful souls in it, who are trying to figure out who they are and how they fit into it.

Unstoppable

An Inspiring Story of an Israeli Actress

Sheena Ray Reynolds

Table of Contents

Introduction 1

Chapter 1 7

Chapter 2 29

Chapter 3 39

Chapter 4 49

Chapter 5 65

Chapter 6 79

Chapter 7 93

Chapter 8 103

Chapter 9 113

Chapter 10 133

Conclusion 149

Introduction

Growing up, I faced many challenges. Every time someone told me I couldn't do something—I only wanted to prove them wrong. I have always felt like a time traveler; I never wanted to be bound and defined by any religion, race, or country. My insecurities were slightly different from the norm since I never felt like I even belonged on this planet. I was insecure about my height, my skin color, my ethnicity, being Jewish, and Israeli. But at some point, I didn't need external love and approval once I realized that the only person whose love I truly needed was my own. Since then, I've felt more free.

That realization was a major inner conversation I had for most of my life. But when I started working on myself, I realized that when you work on your inner self, everything on the outside begins to align. I'm still working on it. I don't think life is a process where you just go to therapy and that's it. I believe we are our own best therapists, and the work is never-ending. You need to work on yourself until the day you die. Otherwise, you'll never be in a growth paradigm. It's not something you do once and then move on.

It sounds horrible, but for most of my life, I felt like a victim of circumstances. I was born prematurely, weighing only 600 grams (about

1.32 pounds). My dad went to jail for murder when I was three and a half. I've faced death a few times and lost a few people who were very close to me when I came to America and was struggling to make it.

During my early childhood years, my dad was labeled a murderer, and people talked about the scars on my hand that I tried so hard to hide. Finally, at one point, I came to the realization that if I had gone through all of these things and overcome so many hardships during my journey to America and my journey to success, I couldn't let anything stop me. I had to be stronger.

I decided to write a book for my healing, and for others, because I know so many other individuals had horrible childhoods that trouble them in their adult lives. Many times, it affects their ability to find love, be in healthy relationships, raise children, accept gifts or love, or just be able to be themselves when around people. They often end up with people who are like their abusers—narcissistic or manipulative—because they're so desperate for love. I wrote this book to help people, and also put it out into the world that this is who I am.

With all the subconscious work I've done, I've been able to change so many things in my life through manifesting, meditating, and changing and growing from within. I came from rough beginnings and have overcome so much. Even though I chased my dream and eventually achieved my lifelong dream of becoming a successful actress, I always felt empty inside. At one point, I finally made the decision to discover who I really was and learn how to love myself without the reassurance of my mother, my sister, my ex-husband, or my son.

I was strong for so many years. I didn't let people abuse or take advantage of me in my adult life. I was very cautious. I shut down and didn't let anyone touch me until I really got to know them, trusted them, and knew they loved me. On top of that, being an Israeli with Middle Eastern, Arabic, Russian, Black, and White grandparents came with a tremendous amount of judgment. Never feeling connected to one part of my ethnicity over the other was quite confusing as a child.

However, as an adult, I gave myself permission to blend in, no matter what part of the world I was living in. Because my self-identity had never been solidified, I was open-minded, which was a good thing, but I still felt very lonely at times. People judged me before they even gave me a chance to speak. I wanted to provide an opportunity for people who come from similar situations and try to make a change for them if they are moving to a new country, and being judged for things that they cannot help. We don't choose where we are born, our skin tone, the language we speak, or who our parents are. It became my goal to help others heal with an open mind.

As I meditated and struggled on my own journey, I realized there were so many organizations out there for women, immigrants, children in need, and even cancer patients, but there's no organization for people who haven't resolved their inner trauma issues to be able to function in society without fear. When I say "without fear," I'm talking about people who are educated, physically capable of working, and decent-looking but still don't function to their fullest potential. Emotionally, there is a block. I could easily have been one of those people. When I look at them, I can't help but imagine how their life would look if they were free of this emotional block and childhood trauma.

It's a challenge because, as humans, we have an innate fear of change. Once we realize that our fear of change is only a survival mechanism, we can ditch the instinct to immediately see someone changing as a bad thing, and instead see change as the beautiful opportunity for growth that it is.

While change starts on the inside, it can be influenced by external factors as well. It's one reason I began my cosmetics business and fell in love with the art of cosmetic injectables. I couldn't help but notice that when I helped clients change their appearance in the physical world, I was simultaneously helping them connect with themselves in the spiritual world through their inner conversations and subconscious mind. It's a balancing act between these two worlds, and it's so beautiful to witness.

What I have discovered is that what the subconscious actually believes can be way more beneficial than years of therapy. I've had women share how deeply it pains them that their husbands don't love them anymore. They looked in the mirror and didn't see themselves anymore; all they saw was the reflection of an old woman. These same women felt being "ugly" made them unlovable, but with a minor beauty enhancement, and a singular, heartfelt conversation with me, I felt as if I was sending them back home a brand new woman, inside and out, one by one.

What's crazy is that when they felt beautiful again, they felt desirable again, and most importantly, they felt loved by their husbands again. My theory just goes to show how powerful our minds, thoughts, and innermost feelings are. Just by changing a single physical feature, their innermost feelings about themselves changed, and when they believed they were beautiful again, others did, too. I see both worlds because I've lived both worlds—from feeling ugly to feeling worthy of love. I intimately understand this journey through and through.

By no means am I claiming that feeling ugly is the biggest struggle in society! It's simply an example of how easy it is for that void to take over. It goes for every struggle in life: if we don't get the help we need, we will never change and never grow. We will be forever stuck with this void as it grows deeper and deeper. Many people in relationships and marriages cheat because they feel a void, or they can't raise their children because they have unresolved issues.

I know we're not perfect; we're only human. We don't get a manual on how to function as human beings, and we're all just doing the best we can. But take it from me: the best thing we can do for ourselves and our loved ones is to heal first. It's the only way to stop carrying the void and passing it on to others. It might feel selfish, but it'll only help you shine and bring more light into the world.

This book is for everyone who wants to look at the small details in life and maybe see something in themselves they can change. It's for those who have faced obstacles and are still struggling, even though they might have a nice house, nice clothes, and a picture-perfect family. Deep down, they're struggling with issues that started early in their childhood and haven't been resolved. I want to tell them that everything is solvable. You can live with the pain beside you—you may never forget, but it's solvable. There's always a way to change. If it doesn't work in one place, it can work in another. You can make mistakes, but most of the time, you can also change things. There's always a start if you decide to do something right with it.

CHAPTER 1

"To understand life better, I had to put it out to the world, so everything will make sense to me first."

Years ago, under the rainy sky, I stood in a long line in Israel to visit my dad in prison. I spent my time waiting in a long line, examining my surroundings. Alongside me were Palestinian wives, mothers, sons, and daughters, all waiting, just like me. Although we were different in the prison line, we were the same. In that line, under the rainy sky, religion, color, or status were nonexistent. It didn't matter if the families surrounding me were eagerly waiting to see their criminal fathers who had caused harm by bombing buildings, hijacking buses, smuggling, or murdering innocents because, despite our differences, we all shared the same feeling. Together, we waited, longing to see our fathers.

As we inched closer to the prison entrance, the reality of the situation weighed heavily on my mind. The line moved slowly, each step reminding me of the reason for our presence there. Despite the discomfort of the cold and wet weather, the solidarity shared among the individuals waiting to see their family members provided a sense of unity and understanding. The atmosphere was solemn, yet there was an unspoken bond that transcended the differences and tragedies that had brought us to this place together.

The process was exhausting, painful, and humiliating. We were stripped of our clothing, had our bags thoroughly checked, and answered numerous questions. Then, we waited in a large room for a long time before being led to another area for about fifteen minutes. If the prison didn't even care to treat us as if we were still human beings, they most certainly could not care less about our ethnicities. Muslim women ahead of us were degraded just as much as anyone else, forced to remove their layers of clothing, including their hijabs. These moments have stuck with me forever, especially after traveling the world and realizing that such treatment doesn't exist anywhere else.

At the time, I didn't know how to explain myself or express what I felt, so I would just observe for most of my childhood. It's like I was stuck between two worlds: the world inside my head and the world outside. You'd be surprised how deeply the experiences in our childhood affect who we are today. As children, our minds are like clay, waiting to be molded. Each experience, in addition to how we react to that experience, forms coping mechanisms that we might still carry with us as adults. Sometimes, we become so used to the things we had to endure during our childhood that we begin to think it is normal, until we are shown otherwise. So, while I knew that a lot of experiences didn't feel right, I didn't know how to express how wrong they really were because at the end of the day, I was just a child.

Upon finally entering the prison walls, a mix of emotions swirled inside me as I anticipated seeing my dad after the long wait. The visitation room had a bittersweet atmosphere, filled with both hope and sadness. Despite the circumstances, the connection between family members remained strong as ever. My heart nearly skipped a beat when I finally reunited with my father. As I sat across from my dad, our conversation was not one you would expect from a criminal. He spent his moments advising me, in detail, what I needed to do to help make this difficult time easier for my mother.

His words were powerful, and I cherished every moment. He complimented my young, smart, and curious mind as he recommended books I should consider reading. He also reminded me of the enduring power of familial love, even in the face of adversity and hardship. He was a *very* special person, and it broke my heart to know that my dad truly didn't deserve to sit in that prison. But through my father, I learned a very important lesson that stayed with me for the rest of my life: no picture is perfect, and when one seems perfect, it may only be a carefully painted illusion. I could have easily slapped a criminal label on my father, but I knew him through and through—I knew his story, and I knew his heart. I learned that the outside image of a person is almost never the full picture. How was it that the "picture-perfect" adults I knew outside of those prison walls were the most sick and twisted, while my father was the kindest soul I knew?

I remember a woman named Rachel and a guy who worked at the prison as a secretary. They were so sweet and human, always saying nice words and treating us with respect, even when others didn't. Some guards treated us terribly, but these two always acted kindly. It was all because of my mom's talent for dealing with people. She knew how to be nice and to give compliments, and she baked them homemade cookies and brought them things. She was very smart. She knew how to navigate that place because her lover, her husband, was there. She would do anything for him, and I admired that about her. She knew it would pay off in the long run—they would treat us a little better than they treated others.

Between these walls, there was no race, religion, terrorist, or murderer. We were all just kids visiting our fathers; all in the same circle, the same agony, the same pain. We didn't know that when we grew up, we might be enemies or we might be friends. At that point, I was exposed to this world, these people, and this specific attitude. And every time I listen to a certain type of music, I cry because it brings me back to that moment, to that little clueless girl who didn't know anything.

I developed an interest in observing people for hours just to absorb and learn from them. I could tell who was embarrassed to visit their father in jail, who felt natural in that environment, who treated the guards like they worked for them, and who enjoyed humiliating people because they felt humiliated themselves.

Sometimes, the guards would check us really deeply. As a little kid, it was like a punch in the gut. They had to check everyone—even kids—because prisoners tried to pass knives, drugs, money, and other things. Many people used their kids for this. I didn't know how to put it into words, but the guards' body language was so obvious—we were the underdogs, the trash, the nothing. They treated us like cattle.

Even though I did nothing wrong as a child—*nothing*—I was scared. I was scared of people in uniforms, scared of being arrested myself, scared of people's faces. I always saw how men looked at my mom like predators because she was so gorgeous. And even though my mom was strong and mostly protected us, just seeing my dad for half an hour was agony, pain, and fear. But then, after all that agony, you'd sit in a beautiful place that looked like a nonchalant coffee shop in West Hollywood with tables, coffee, tea, and nice things to eat from the store there, and my mom would pay for that.

We'd sit in a nice yard, play with other kids, and everything looked beautiful. But it was so exhausting for a little kid. You don't know how to explain the conversation in your head because it's your norm. You don't know anything else, so this is what gets plugged into your subconscious as a little kid. That's why it took me so many years to change my subconscious, and I want to teach others that it is possible.

Every visit to my dad developed the hope that maybe he'd come home soon. It gave me a little optimism for a better future. Maybe we'd be a family with a dad, mom, sister, and a little dog in a beautiful little house. I pictured everything down to the tiniest details.

In the winter, it was so cold you could feel it in your bones, trudging through the mud with your shoes soaked. And in the summer, it was so hot you felt sticky all over your body. And I always thought about my dad. Was he hot at night? Was someone covering him? Did he have a blanket? Would he ever read me a story again? I know it sounds cliché and dramatic, like something out of a movie, but when you don't have peace of mind as a little kid, it stumps your creativity and your ability to imagine a future. You can't imagine, envision, or have dreams like normal kids. You have no space to create because all your energy is dedicated to your survival. Your mind isn't butterflies and rainbows; it's a survival-mode prison, fighting to survive all the chaos in your mind. This is the time when the subconscious needs to build a vision for the future, and I didn't have that opportunity as a little kid. For half of my life, I needed to fix myself just to be like a normal person and start to create.

So, on this visit, I felt happy because I had a dad. But when I got home, I needed to find comfort in his letters. His letters were beautiful, decorated with pink paper. He'd write, *"I hope you do your homework; I hope you listen to your mom. Mommy's working so hard. You really have to understand her and help her."* His letters were very direct about what to do and what not to do and very optimistic, with a shiny, glittery vision of the future. Dad always had an analytical mind and a talent for writing. He exposed me to Socrates, Aristotle, Plato, Carl Jung, and other great writers. He'd teach me how to speak better, and the way he spoke was amazing—I loved listening to him.

Sometimes, he'd call in the evening and talk to me before I went to sleep. I used to fall asleep with his letters beside me, crying and waiting for the next one. He always had beautiful sentences that made me think. *"Never lie because only the truth you can remember." "Remember, when you're in a stressful situation, think before you act. It's really important to take a breath for a second."* We always had great intellectual debates. He taught me that, at the end of the day, we were all just human beings. We had titles like Arab, Jew, White, and Black, but at the end of the day, we were all human. We didn't need to segregate or give titles to everything. I learned a lot from him. He was always there in the background, giving me guidance, even if he wasn't physically home. He was very intelligent and had so much integrity.

We'd get ready, excited to go see my dad. I saw how organized and clean my mom was. She was very straight to the point—working, saving, and having a specific budgeted amount, every month, to give my dad so he wouldn't miss anything in prison. They had a great love—I used to call them "Bonnie and Clyde." He was her man, and she would do whatever it took to wait for him because she was devoted. She'd married him and would never divorce him. She'd stick with him through thick and thin, for better or worse, in sickness and health, because she'd made a vow when they got married. She always told him that. So, that being said, I admired her, but I was also afraid of her. She never thought of leaving him. They had a love like in the movies. The kids were just part of the stunts in their own show, in their own film. At least, that's how I felt. We'd wake up in the middle of the night because we had to hide from the family of the person my dad killed. This family was gang-affiliated. My mom was always calm, always spoke calmly and with calculation, explaining everything down to the last detail. She was more impulsive, acting from her gut, and this is how they matched each other—like a good cop, bad cop.

When I was a kid—I was a different kind of kid—I didn't know how to see my mom for who she really was. Her demeanor was tough. She had a masculine energy. She was not nurturing—at all. She was always on a mission: fighting the system, surviving, working, constantly doing. As a child, I couldn't understand that.

Only now, after time has passed, after becoming a single mom myself—having to survive and go against everything—have I finally started to see her in a different light. The glimmers of understanding have begun to appear before my eyes.

She was never nurturing, never kissing, never hugging—never the kind of mom who said, "Come, let me make you food. I love you"—growing up like that was difficult. I couldn't understand her. Then, when I looked at her history—what she endured as a child, waiting fifteen years for her husband while he was in jail, remaining completely faithful and loyal to him, to her family, to the very structure of *family* itself—I began to admire her. But I also felt sorry for her. Not just as a grown woman, but as the child she once was. As the woman I saw from the sidelines—a fighter, trying to be there for her husband and kids no matter what.

I couldn't understand it back then. Because all of us, including myself, are self-absorbed in our own pain, in our own lives. That's human nature—we're born into our individual bodies, with individual minds, and we see the world from our own perspectives. But when you step outside of that, when you absorb life from a broader view, it becomes easier to open your mind and have compassion for people, and your mother. Even if she hit you. Even if she got mad at you. Even if, because she saw you as strong, she sometimes took out her stress on you.

I finally understood because, many times, I find my mother in myself. In some ways, I am nothing like her—I was a nurturing mother. I parented out of guilt. I gave my son more than I was supposed to, more than I even had to give.

But in other ways, I was just like her. A fighter. Someone who never gave up. And I realized—that's what made me resilient.

Today, when I compare women of different generations to my mom's generation, I see how different things are. No woman today would wait fifteen years for her husband, still love him, still stand by him, and still do everything for him. I learned from my mother and my family the meaning of loyalty, of never leaving anyone behind.

That's how we say it in Hebrew, you don't leave the people you love behind. Not for comfort. Not for money. Not for anything. You stay. You do whatever it takes to protect your family, your husband, your kids. You don't "air your dirty laundry in public." Family values are stronger than anything.

And I couldn't see it before.

Even though I have my criticisms, things my mother could have done differently, the most important thing is understanding that no one is perfect.

We don't get a manual when we become parents. And what makes us extraordinary is not focusing on what we didn't get, on what someone wasn't, on what went wrong, but instead, choosing to see the good. Choosing to see the cup as half full.

That's what I do. With family, with friends, with everyone. I always choose to see the good in people rather than the bad. Because at any moment, God can put us in the same shoes as the people we once judged.

And even though this way of thinking gets me into trouble, because people assume I'm weak or easy to push around, I know it's what makes me unique. I see life through a different lens. I see people for who they truly are, rather than judging them for how they want the world to perceive them.

I remember my mother's perfume. She was beautiful, like Farrah Fawcett, and very classy. She would go to visit her love, prepare us with sweet smells and beautiful clothes, and say, "I don't want anybody to feel sorry for you. I don't want you to miss anything: clothes, food, anything." She married my father because he was smart, interesting, and articulate—a person she could talk to and learn from. She always loved and admired him. She also told me that before he got arrested, he was very jealous; he loved her and was a little protective. She had a difficult time with him. But she had been with him since she was sixteen. She strongly believed that one should never "leave their troop in combat." I think it's a good thing in a way; she never left her lover. She's from a generation where if something breaks, you don't throw it away; you fix it. She was completely loyal to him, but it was a different kind of loyalty.

My mom came from a place where she didn't have her own space. She had to struggle from an early age. They made her live with her older brother and be a slave, taking care of the kids and doing everything, from the age of eight. Her mom was married to her father, and her father was married to two women: her mom and her cousin. Between them, they had almost twenty kids, and she had a traumatic childhood. She came from a place where she didn't have a mother's love. So sometimes, I would think, how can I resent her? She couldn't give me what she didn't have. She was a Jewish woman born in an Arab country (Morocco) who had to emigrate to Israel. She lived in a house as an immigrant, where she had to fight for her spot, and for her father's love, because they had two families in the same house. I absorbed all this as a little kid, but when I grew up, I finally opened my eyes and saw her as a woman who was still a little girl.

When I had compassion, I had a mechanism. When you're from a culture of resentment, you can deal with it. Instead of hate or resentment, you can feel compassion, and then you understand. If you're smart, this is the right way. You don't hate people for what they cannot do. You just feel sorry for them and for yourself because, well, this is the only way that makes sense to me. I cannot hate people for what they've done. You have to forgive. This is the only way to heal yourself and the world—*you forgive*.

Where I come from, forgiving and forgetting was unheard of. Some of the kids came from parents who were in crime families. For some of the kids, it was completely normal. Their psychological identity was tied to the respect they got in the street just because of their uncle, father, or cousin. "My uncle is this." "My father is that." They would come and threaten you with this and that, squeezing people for this or that because they were supposedly the celebs of crime families. And as much as it sounds absurd to regular people, for them, it was a source of pride. This was who they were, and this was who they looked up to in their childhood. And I absorbed it, but I realized you're going to look up to a gangster who drives a nice car and has diamonds, if he is the only successful person in your neighborhood. If you grew up in a family where everyone was a banker or a doctor, that was who you were going to look up to. This is what gets placed in our subconscious as we grow up, and most people don't know that. They don't even realize they're looking up to the wrong people because it's what surrounds them.

Sometimes, I was just there absorbing it, realizing some of these people were really, really bad. I felt really bad for some of them. Some were the second or third generation in crime, and you could see who was going to follow their father or brother, who was mistakenly there, and who was there because they had no soul when you looked into their eyes. I was studying body language so intently that I learned to understand people. I could talk to someone for two minutes and already know what was up with them. I already knew who was going to try to abuse me and who was good.

I realized that most people there didn't get love, didn't have parents who accepted them or didn't have society's acceptance. They acted on autopilot, raising kids by the norms they knew, growing up in their specific group, and never reaching outside of their comfort zone. And I learned to recognize them. Naturally, interactions happened because they were there, and I was bored. I didn't want to interact with them, but I had no choice because I was already there. My language was different from theirs because I was reading books, being exposed to different worlds, in a good school, and singing opera. They thought I was going to be a very good opera singer. But I was still in this loop of a crime family and visiting my dad in jail, even though my perception of life was completely different. I felt like a stranger in a dirty environment.

But I still remember the Palestinian kids holding their babies with mucus on their faces, swatting the flies away with their hands while the babies screamed. Every time I hear a baby cry, I remember the Palestinian babies waiting in line with us, with sad faces, and the mothers looking at me like I was the enemy because I was in between both worlds. The screaming in Arabic, the screaming in Ethiopian, the screaming in Hebrew from the people who didn't get what they wanted. Hearing all these languages around me, everything was so chaotic. We'd sit for hours, like flies, waiting for the guard. It was really, really traumatic for me.

I realized that I was like a magician. I had all this power to create characters for myself. I go to the jail, and I have to deal with these specific people there. I go to school, and I'm a completely different person. I go to my opera lessons and play the piano. I'm a good kid who plays the piano and sings opera. And then, in front of other people, they ask me, "Is your daddy a murderer?" So, I realized I was a different person inside, and I had to play the game outside because society could be so vicious. People only see what they want to see based on the physical image in front of them. They see ten percent and automatically assume the other ninety percent. But thank God, most of my close friends, even though I didn't have many, were very intelligent: just a group of dorks, deep, and interested in art and literature.

When I visited the jail, I had to play with other children who were also on visits. Sometimes, we couldn't visit my dad because he was in detention. It fueled my imagination. He would speak of his living conditions, about how he had no mattress or blanket. He'd tell us these stories. My parents would talk about everything in front of us. I used to write about it just to comprehend it.

My curiosity to understand people, human beings, and mainly my parents, even though I had all this emotional pain and stress, always led me to try to understand the root of the problem, where it all went wrong, and when it all started, just to try to fix it. I became the person who corrects everything. It didn't matter if I was injecting people and doing superficial work—I was always specializing in correcting scars, dysmorphia, whatever you call it. If I did meditation, I wanted to correct the woman who'd been raped, the woman who didn't feel good on the inside. I was always taking the role of someone who needs to correct, who needs to fix. Because every time I corrected other people, I realized maybe it was not their fault—maybe they had bad parents. I wanted to understand them.

But then I realized something else. From the day we are born until we are seven years old, our mind absorbs everything like a sponge and then stores it like the hard drive of a computer. The subconscious is the program of the brain. When we are babies, we start to analyze, break down the software, and collect information and data. We learn how to have relationships, how to love, how to react, and how to act. The brain learns from a very early age how to be obsessive, violent, good, bad, compassionate, and gentle. The subconscious rehearses everything, one after the other. The subconscious will rehearse the things that bothered and disturbed us, and the trauma we have experienced. The activity of the brain and the data it absorbs starts even from seven months in the womb. We have to remember that ninety percent of our life is on autopilot. It comes from the subconscious.

If you look at the life of a normal person, you can understand in a single scenario what is embedded in their heart and how it operates on that subconscious automatic pilot that took hold from the age of seven—if you're smart enough and know how to absorb it. You can see how these traumas and patterns from childhood carry into adult life. Most of the time, if a girl was raped, she might be drawn to abusive men who would continue to abuse her, even if she didn't realize it. It was in her subconscious, plugged into the hard drive of her mind. This was how she learned about love, and she believed this was the correct kind of love because it was the only "love" she knew.

If someone was spoiled as a little kid, they may not develop properly because they always feel entitled, as if the world owes them something. They might have a chip on their shoulder, wanting to use, manipulate, lie, and avoid responsibility, even as an adult. This is how humans can drive this automatic violence without understanding the machine or the heart they were born with—without knowing how they were programmed, who programmed them, or that they are merely a program. It's not really them; they can change that program and become a different person. To become a different person, we really have to change that program and become a different part of the world.

And people, the human cattle, need a community, the support of other human beings, and feedback, visual feedback, emotional feedback, mental feedback, conversation, to live in a society. The global mindset of most people is like cattle. They follow the herd. If something is fashionable, they want to be part of it. They learn what other people learn, and they don't want to be different. The majority, I believe ninety-five percent, of people are like this, and it's very difficult to change that because when you're already old, the hard drive is set; it's already there, deep within. Most humans live in this magical vicious cycle.

I understood what I'd been through and how I was locked into the program. In order to change the program, you need to step outside yourself. It's like you're baking a cake, and you have all the ingredients in front of you, and you think about how you're going to bake it. So, I had to put all the ingredients in front of me and say, *Okay, I've been mentally abused. I've been physically abused. I've been emotionally abused. I grew up around abusive people, in and out of jails. How is this going to affect me? How am I going to prevent this from affecting me? What's the next step?* I'm a person of solutions, not a person of problems. How do I reach a solution? How do I take that person they call Sheena and make her the best version of herself as a woman who can physically and emotionally function successfully in society? A woman who doesn't operate on automatic pilot, or take all that pain and act from that wounded child?

To do that, I had to hit rock bottom, become homeless, and start to create from nothing, because I had to put my ego aside and really understand that a problem is not just a problem; every problem has a root, something much deeper than it seems. And if you're lying to yourself, blaming others, and not taking accountability and responsibility, you'll never understand who you are and what ingredients made you—shaped you. But the moment you start to understand yourself, it's not going to happen in one day. You have to meditate every day. You have to have conversations with yourself every day. You have to catch yourself in the middle of a conversation with others and say to yourself, *Don't say this, don't be jealous, don't be scared, don't be afraid to stand up for your rights.* And I had to do this every day without being afraid. Then, I would go home and write, putting it all on paper.

I didn't want to tell people that I was working on myself because I was worried they would think I was crazy, talking to myself, and trying to correct myself on a daily basis. Correcting yourself and working on yourself is not about going to a psychologist for a few months, a year, or seven years and then thinking you're fixed and a new person. We really have to make the program new, and when you make the program new, slowly but surely, you become more resilient. You understand things better, you're not impulsive, and you think before you speak. You give opportunities to yourself and to others. You learn not to judge people because of their color, religion, or looks—because they don't look clean or because of how they eat.

As humans, we are very judgmental. We always have problems with something. We can be nice to some people, but most people, at the end of the day, are a bit selfish. Most people are narcissistic to some extent. The only difference is that some people know how to hide it, how to play with it, and how to put it in the right proportions. We are all here in the game of life, and the more you play that game correctly and understand yourself better, the easier it will be for you to walk the journey of life.

You have a few things you can bargain with: your ego, which plays an important role, your respect, and the allowance you receive. And they are acting like animals in a cage. In the "jungle" of prison, but inside a cage. You see, the wives came to prison with a twisted mindset. They think they are collaborating with power, but they don't understand that the majority of criminals come from a very weak place, mentally. These are people who used to live in survival mode. Many of them don't stop for a minute to think about the consequences of their actions. There's a specific type of woman who really likes it this way—they love criminals, and love the crime world because they love the feeling of power. As a little kid, I saw them showing up in large groups. I even saw a prisoner who had a rotation of women coming between visits.

A lot of women out there need a man. Even if the man doesn't live with her, she just needs to know that she has a man who can call her, write letters to her, talk to her, email her, whatever it is. But the majority of women, even though they say they're strong and resilient, do need to have a man who is with them. The fact of the matter is, it makes them a slave—to the relationship, to the system, to their mentality, and to who they are.

As a little kid growing up next to serial killers (bumping into them, if that's the right word) and I didn't fully grasp the gravity of it or what it truly meant. I didn't understand the impact of what they did, even though I felt it, without fully processing it.

Looking back on that story, I remember one serial killer: his body language, the way he spoke to me, and how others treated him. It terrified me because I was about the same age as the child he killed. What unsettles me even more is realizing how reckless and irresponsible my parents were—sitting at the table, having their own conversation, while I unknowingly interacted with him. They weren't afraid, nor were they even watching me. That thought has stayed with me over the years.

Reflecting on my life as if watching a documentary in reverse has made me realize that I need to live differently, especially for my son. I must take responsibility for every decision I make, always considering the outcome before taking action. My experiences being around murderers, rapists, and criminals, even those imprisoned for political violence like bombings, shaped my understanding of people. Observing their voices, demeanor, and body language, and later traveling and seeing people from different cultures and mentalities, gave me the perspective to recognize how my upbringing could have led me down a dangerous path.

When you grow up surrounded by such people, you naturally mimic them. To break that cycle, one needs an outside perspective and the ability to question everything. Fortunately, I had that instinct—thank God.

Even now, when I see someone with a particular look on their face, it takes me back, like a scene in a movie where fragments of the past flash before the character's eyes, revealing why they are the way they are. I often experience that same comparison.

One day, I went to the prison to visit my dad. We were sitting in a nice place that was almost like sitting in a restaurant. All these prisoners were walking around, but I remember one precisely. He had oily skin, was bald with a little hair on the side, and was very ugly. His name was Tzvi Gur.

He'd kidnapped a little boy, Oron Yarden, and wrapped him so tightly in carpet that he'd died of suffocation and neglect. It was a very famous story in all the newspapers. We saw it on the news. Even as a child, I saw everything on TV. When we went to jail, we saw him in person. So, every time I visited, I saw him walking around the jail. I said to myself, *I seriously can't stand this guy. Simply the thought of him annoys me.* Yet, I still asked him questions, so that I could write his answers in my journal.

One day, I approached him, and I realized my dad was his protector because everyone wanted to beat him up for murdering a child. But because this guy was a White Ashkenazi Jew, and my dad was the only guy who really read books in jail, and this guy read books too, they collaborated. My dad said he'd protect him, and the guy worked in the library, providing my dad with books. He was also an artist and knew how to paint very well, so he painted a few pictures that my mom hung in the living room. One was of a mother, father, two daughters, a dog, and a bird symbolizing freedom. And I saw this painting every day in my house, and I resented my parents for putting it up.

On one visit, I saw him there, and I was bored. So, I walked up to him and said, "Hey, can I ask you a question? I'm writing this journal, and I want to know something. You're Tzvi."

He replied, "Yeah."

So, I asked, "How did you feel the moment you realized he died? Did you feel something? Did you feel bad?"

I saw his face turn pale, like a nine-year-old kid who'd been caught doing something wrong. He was so embarrassed, and I could see the sweat forming under his nose. He looked at me, sweating, and his eyes said, *Why is she asking me this?* I asked him if he felt guilty, if he would do things differently today, or if he would change what he did. But he didn't answer. He just stared at me, not knowing what to do. Then he asked, "Why are you asking so many questions? Who told you this story?"

I told him, "I saw it on the news."

That's when I realized he'd met my best friend—conscience. Conscience is my best friend. It goes with me everywhere. Everything I do, I do it out of conscience. And he'd met his conscience for the first time. I could see it in his eyes that he'd finally faced his conscience and didn't know how to handle it. That was a very profound moment for me: understanding that I was watching a murderer finally meet his conscience in real time. He didn't know what conscience was before because nobody had ever asked him these questions.

I saw all sorts of famous criminals in this jail. Sometimes, they would come to my mom's house, buy us candy and gifts, put us on their laps, laugh, and smile—just like in a mafia movie. For a while, it was normal for me. But a lot of people were afraid to talk to me, and it was embarrassing. I would go to birthday parties, only to be turned away at the door, even though we had gotten ready, dressed nicely, and bought a nice gift. We weren't allowed into the parties. We had to be isolated.

I grew up with all this, and then when I moved to America, became successful, and made a name for myself, another Israeli woman in my community started spreading rumors about me online. She spread all this bad stuff about me, making me look like a bad person, like a criminal. I've never had a criminal record. I've never owed money to anyone. I've never done anything to break the law. I worked so hard my whole life to be a stand-up person, so no one could ever attach me to my dad's history. Then suddenly, this woman comes and "contaminates" me, which made me relive my childhood trauma. I was questioning my reputation and who I was as a person and mother. I would sit and wonder, *Maybe I'm a bad person, and she's right. Maybe I did do something, and I don't remember. Maybe I'm going crazy. Maybe I am crazy. Maybe she's right. Maybe I'm a scam artist, and I'm running away.*

But then, when I talked to my best friend, she'd say, "Listen, you're going crazy, stop it. It's not you. You're a good person. I've known you since we were twelve. What's wrong with you? You have to snap out of it." It doesn't matter how much work you do—if one crazy person comes into your life, they can flip the coin and bring you back to your old paradigm, just like a drug addict who's been sucked into a relapse.

That's when it occurred to me, and I thought, *You know what? I didn't go through all this in my life, working on myself, working on my inner conversation, writing, going to therapy, going to India, taking meditation classes, and doing all this just for one person to flip the coin and take me back to my old self. I have to be smarter than that.*

My identity was complex from the beginning because my grandfather was Black, Ethiopian, and half-Muslim. My grandmother on my dad's side was the daughter of a Syrian immigrant from Homs. But her father was someone she didn't know. He was a Russian immigrant, probably married, and they'd had an affair, which is how my father was born. So, for starters, my identity was complex. Growing up in Israel, where the main language is Hebrew, the second language is Arabic, and the third is

English, I had to learn all three languages. On my father's side, I'm Arab and Russian, but I didn't know any Russian. I grew up with Russians in my building, but not in my family.

I grew up in a family that speaks fluent Arabic on my dad's side. On my mom's side, she was born in Morocco, an Arab country, but she's Jewish. So, she's Jewish with a strong Arabic and Middle Eastern perspective on things. She brought that mentality, which had its pros and cons, into raising her kids.

In my mom's house, they spoke French, Moroccan, Arabic, Hebrew, and Moroccan-Arabic, so I had to learn five languages. And in my dad's house, they spoke regular Arabic and Hebrew. And my nanny spoke to me in English. English was the most amazing thing because I identified with it. I wanted to be something different. My oasis was Madonna, believe it or not. I decided I wanted to speak English, go to America, and meet Madonna—that was my dream.

When I was seven years old, my uncle taught meditation and yoga in India, so he would come to Israel every few months and bring people from all over the world: India, Amsterdam, London, and all the yogis who traveled with him. They taught us meditation. So, at a very early age, I was exposed to many cultures. When I grew up and became an actress, my specialty was accents and characters. I could be Indian, British, French, Arabic, or Russian and that's why I became such a good actress without going to acting school. But deep down inside, this was my identity crisis—I never felt whole.

Chapter 2

As a child, I waited for letters from my dad because they kept me going. They gave me hope and something to look forward to. As I grew up, I realized that everyone needs hope. If I hadn't received those letters, I wouldn't have had hope or a vision for the future.

Every time I received a letter, it would tell me everything I wanted to hear: *"I will come out, and I will take you to Disney World. I will take you to America. We are going to have a dog and a normal family, and we will ride horses, and I will teach you how to swim."* These letters would help me visualize everything and imagine what a beautiful future could bring, reminding me that even though I was not with my dad, I still had one. These words of affirmation kept me sane as they blocked out the negative feelings. For me, those letters were everything.

In these same letters, he advised me to be vigilant, especially as a woman in this world. I didn't know it at the time, but looking back, this lesson, which I carried with me from an early age, helped me survive as a single woman with a child in the jungle of the world.

I didn't have a husband or someone to protect me. As a woman, I know that as much as we want to be feminists, we need a man to protect us because men are more intimidating physically. I don't want to be overly feminist. I want to be the kind of woman a man can protect. But we need to give men that space. Surround yourself with good men, good family, and good people who protect you rather than who treat you like you're not important.

My dad always explained things to me in detail. He said that in this world, people will always judge you. There's no right way to live life because, for some communities, religion is the right thing; for others, being a professor or a lawyer is the right thing. You can never win. He said to always let people hear what they want to hear and then do what your conscience and mind tell you is the right thing to do. He always gave me these specific tools and guidance. He would say that the majority of people will always want something from you. You need to identify what that something is and utilize it or realize if people are trying to use you for something. And it was better to have one good friend than twenty friends. He knew I had a lot of learning disabilities, and he said, "I know it's hard for you to learn. But remember, education and knowledge are power. The more you know about the world and things, the more power you can have. Just swim freely in this world." I appreciate what he said.

When you're a little girl in this world, it's very chaotic. When he said all these things, I didn't fully understand them at the time. My inner conversation wasn't fully developed, so I couldn't even explain certain things to myself or figure out how to approach certain situations. But as I grew up, year after year, every sentence found its place and started to make sense in my eyes. I realized this was his only way, because he was absent physically, to try to raise me and give me some kind of verbal protection through the letters. I think he was smart because not a lot of dads in his position would go out of their way to write such thorough and deep letters to their daughters.

With what he had, this was the best he could do. I remembered my father's wisdom in countless situations over time. For example, if a guy tried to kiss me by force at school, I would think about what my dad told me. I'd be like, *What am I doing here alone? He told me not to be alone in certain areas. What am I doing here? This is dangerous.* I would never go out in the dark at night or get in an elevator alone—or a lot of other things. I had to develop a huge protection mechanism to avoid getting hurt, dragged, or worse, because of his words.

After the letters, the prison started letting him call the house almost every night. He would say, "Listen, I know you're at the age of puberty, and maybe you want to have sex, but you have to understand there are diseases. You could get pregnant, and it could destroy your whole life." He was the only one who actually talked to me about all these things, and who knows where I would have been without it.

He would explain, "In prison, whether you are Jewish, Muslim, Russian, Arab, Ethiopian, Black, or White, it doesn't matter, here, we're all prisoners. It doesn't matter who you killed. We're all the same. Against the system."

So, if you wanted to have TV, video, music, or good food, you needed to fight the system. And because my dad spoke two languages, it was easy for him to communicate with everyone, and he never had any enemies. Literally, I've never heard anyone say anything bad about my dad. Quite the opposite. People would say, "Sheena! Your father is so amazing. You'd never believe how much he helped me." I met people who spoke with him in jail and said, "If it wasn't for your dad, I wouldn't have eaten. He would split the money your mom gave him. He would buy me things, even cigarettes." Another person said, "Oh, your dad helped me rehab from drugs in jail."

We even had Arabs from Arab villages in Israel tell me, "Just so you know, your dad is my best friend." One time, I was in a club in Tel Aviv, and this guy smacked my butt. An Arab guy who knew my dad was there, and he beat the guy up, saying, "Listen, she's the daughter of my best friend. Don't you dare touch her."

Over the years, I've met people who admire my dad for being such a good person. He never thought about himself; he always thought about how to help other people.

When he was released from jail, you wouldn't believe how many people stayed at our house: people in rehab, those who were homeless, and people who had no place to go. All his life, he was dedicated to helping and giving. That's why I learned that an image is just an image; someone might seem rough on the outside, but deep down, they could be a good person. The full story of him killing someone is actually that he was protecting a person who was getting beaten.

My dad was in a restaurant and saw a guy getting beaten up by younger men. He asked what was going on, and they said, "He owes us protection money and cannot pay."

My dad responded, "Hey, this man could be a father. How could you do this to someone?" And that's how he got involved with the gangsters. They almost killed my dad, but he had to do what he felt was right. So, I grew up with a person who had a good heart, and his mission was to help people. But with that being said, he was always more focused on helping strangers, giving them his time, talking to them, and educating them. When he got out of jail, he never had time for me or my sister, which was the worst. We were so hurt by this. It was like, how can you help all these people, and we are always left behind?

After his release, he finished law school and became a lawyer. I'm not sure if he took the final test, there was some issue with the test or his evaluation, but he almost completed everything. Then he started writing for people, reducing their sentences, believe it or not. He helped people all the time, writing their letters to the Supreme Court, telling them what to say to their lawyers, and how to handle things. He would often say to my mom, "Oh, I'm sorry, I can't talk right now. I have to help this guy; he has a trial next week, and I need to work on these letters." I was in shock. I couldn't believe my dad was doing it. It was amazing, but he did it. He was helping people because he was studying law and became so skilled at it.

One day, he found himself in the prison cell all by himself: no bed, no mattress, no books, nothing. Literally nothing 24/7 for a month. He said he used to do multiplication to keep his mind sharp. When he was a kid, he studied a lot of scripture, though he wasn't religious. He's an atheist and doesn't believe in anything. He would memorize passages from the Bible, write sentences, make plans, and exercise. Every day, he would do about thirty minutes of exercise inside, walking back and forth. He showed me all this when I was a kid. He would hate doing it, but would do it for the greater cause.

The prisoners didn't want to do it under those conditions or live like dogs, but he sett an example for the others. He believed in being a leader rather than a follower. I think that's what made me the way I am. I would take on a lot of bad things for the "team" sometimes, but I wanted to change, help, and guide. I wasn't a coward, and he's not a coward. I'm not afraid of anything, and he's not afraid of anything. So I think I learned that from him in all our deep conversations. We could talk about religion, your state of mind, criminology, everything. In that sense, I think I'm a lot like him.

I could tell his mind and his way of thinking were unique. He had a criminal sitting with him in jail who had killed a lot of Israelis and Jews. And they became very good friends. His Jewish friend got mad at him because the guy was Palestinian. But he said to his friend, "Listen, I know he's a murderer, I know he's Palestinian, but you have to understand, he grew up in a segregated place where Israel was seen as the bad guy. You have to understand that if we have the opportunity to get to know each other, this is what we need to do as humans. Because, above all, before everything else, we are human beings. Before we are Palestinian, Israeli, Black, or White, we are human beings."

He would tell me all these murder stories when I was a kid, and I developed an interest in learning more. These stories didn't scare me—they intrigued me. I grew to love watching real FBI cases. I spent years watching these things, studying patterns, and even writing about them. I even questioned myself: *Could I be a killer?* If I had the ability to hurt someone, would I do it if I had no choice? I pondered that question for years.

At the end of the day, when I think about it, I realize I could never hurt someone unless they were trying to hurt my son, my family, or me, and I really had no choice. In that situation, I would do it. But I would never want to deal with that because the emotional burden you carry after killing someone is not something that money, circumstances, or anything else can fix. It's something that would live within you for the rest of your life.

I've seen my dad wrestling with this guilt. I think that's why he never actually speaks to God. It's easier for him to be an atheist. I don't know if he's an atheist because he's very intelligent and has a highly scientific, logical way of thinking. He's not driven by crazy emotions. So, I'm not sure if it's because of that or because he developed a protection mechanism to shield his soul from hurt, fear, or really confronting those questions.

I dealt with that "could I be a killer" question for a year, trying to understand if I'm like that. That's the reason I avoided staying in the army and participating because I didn't want to confront that question. It's not that I believe the Israeli army would go kill people; that's simply not its protocol. I've never met a soldier who would do that if it wasn't in the name of protection. But I'm not saying there aren't people like that; there could be. But the majority are not like that, and I know that one hundred percent.

Most importantly, we are human. You're not Palestinian, you're not Black, you're not Jewish—you're a human being. And when you're killing and taking the life of another human being, do you understand how crazy and heavy that is? People don't grasp it. They go into automatic violence in the name of religion, war, or hate. But at the end of the day, we are human beings. That's it. It doesn't matter if it's the Inquisition, World War II, slavery, civil war, Palestine, Israel, or whatever, we are all human beings deciding to take the lives of others, and we are not allowed to do that.

That's the most important message we need to bring to the world. Before you say, "Palestine is my country, are you occupied?" or "This is Israel, and it's my land since biblical times," no matter what your point of view, you have to understand—this is planet Earth. We should all live together, get along, and love each other because we have nothing besides each other for human comfort. We are all going to live and die one day, all of us together. And just because we're all going to die one day, which is our common denominator, we should love and support each other, walking together on that path toward death instead of executing each other along the way.

Growing up with a dad who was sitting in jail for murder was tricky. On the one hand, he was gentle and understanding, writing me thoughtful letters, offering advice, and talking with me about serious books, science, humanity, and how to be a good person who never lies. He even taught me how to carry myself when I'm among men. But then, in the visitation room, I saw men who looked completely different—vicious, with some faces that looked like rapists, or at least like hunters, like someone always looking for something, you know? And that's what I saw as a little kid.

Then, when you grow up and step into the world, you meet men who seem completely different—men who appear sweet and soft on the outside, but behind closed doors, they act vicious—worse than a lot of the criminals I met, right? So I found myself speaking freely with my dad, coming to him and actually talking about these things. I even asked him: "How did you feel after you shot the guy? How do you feel emotionally? What do you think you're going to be punished for? Do you think you're going to hell?" We went very, very deep in our conversations. And my dad always told me that things are not how they seem. He said he would never take another person's life unless it was something truly inevitable.

Of course, that's not an excuse for anything. But he taught me—and that's when I started to understand why he always made it a point to teach me how to act around men. And instead of growing up hating men, that's actually the reason I'm doing all these podcasts, advocating for men, and speaking so positively about them. Because I know, as women—and especially as feminist women—we're often taught to hate men, to always look for the bad ones, to point fingers at the "bad guys."

We have to remember that the majority of men in the world are hardworking. There are good men out there who genuinely want to be nurturing, to treat women well, and to protect them—because, at their core, they are protectors. Rotating between these two worlds—seeing men at their worst and then meeting men at their best—taught me how to read body language, and how to understand the unspoken. And it reminded me of something I said earlier: we're all, in a way, just sponges—absorbing the environment we grew up in.

We're all, in some way, a sponge of what we witnessed in our childhood. And for a woman to grow into a good woman—or a man to grow into a good man—there needs to be a strong example. There needs to be emotional support from the opposite sex.

You need to see good examples at home—how your dad treats your mom, how he treats others, how your mom responds, and how she treats your dad. That's where I learned a lot about loyalty.

My mom didn't ditch my dad or just go live her life. She waited for him. She taught me what loyalty, consistency, and commitment to a journey really mean. She knew her husband was going to prison for many years, but still, she stood by him. She worked hard and did whatever needed to be done so they could walk that path together.

As a kid, I used to think, *Oh, she's stupid for waiting for him.* But we live life moving forward and understand it looking backward. And now, with the outer perspective of an adult looking back at that little girl, I get it. I understand the journey. I understand the process.

I learned what loyalty truly means. And when I speak in front of people today, I realize that this part of my life taught me so much—about the good and the bad in people, especially in men. I can see through men in a way many women can't—not because I'm trying to make them my boyfriend or husband, or because I think all men are bad—but because I understand the child in them. I understand what shaped them, and why they become who they are—for better or worse.

And even though it was a really scary and unique journey, as a grown woman, I'm actually grateful for it. Because now, I see things that a lot of people don't. My perspective is completely different. It's expansive—global, even—because I've lived and understood both sides of the equation. I don't just see one angle; I see the full picture.

Chapter 3

I never had a sense of belonging to anybody or any place. I never felt at home anywhere. Wherever my bed was, that was my home. If I had a good bed, a clean bed, a nice blanket, that was my home. I never really felt a sense of belonging. I never really felt Jewish, Christian, Muslim—nothing. So, the sense of belonging was completely off. I never felt like I had a home. I decided that because I didn't feel it, I needed to create my own home. And if there's one thing I was gonna do, it was to keep my word. Because if you can't trust yourself, who are you gonna trust?

I discovered that I had no problem traveling as a fifteen or sixteen-year-old by myself, flying to a brand new country, not knowing anybody. I was confident with my lone travels, and my self-esteem reached new levels. This is where I learned the power of experience, trial and error in relation to our self-esteem. The best way to build your self-esteem is to build a relationship with yourself. Discover yourself as if you were meeting a person for the first time, without all the self-doubt and second-guessing.

With each new place I traveled, new person I met, and new experience I experienced, my perspective expanded. There was no room for self-doubt or second-guessing anymore because any time my mind went there, I had evidence to show for it. The thought that I had created the person I am today was all the evidence I needed to support my self-esteem, and that confidence shifted everything. I'll tell you what the secret was. When I was twelve and a half, I started working. I realized that when I worked, even though I went to school, I had pocket money.

When I had money, I had freedom. For example, if I went out with a bunch of fourteen-year-olds to a movie, they all had to ask their parents for money. I always had my own money. I had a lot of self-esteem. I could go out and not need to ask for money because I was working. I always found jobs, like babysitting or cleaning, and I always had that ability to create, which gave me a lot of confidence.

When I was ten years old, we moved to a high-end area in Tel Aviv, which was all White Ashkenazi Jews. I was singing opera, and I felt a much lower self-esteem. For example, in the choir, because my voice was soprano, they loved my voice, but they had to put me at the end. The teacher came and said, "You're too dark, you're too short, and your hair is too frizzy. You have to be at the end of the choir, in the second row. You're not front-row material." Even though her words were like a punch in the face, it was sentences like these that gave me the raging desire and burning motivation to keep going and build my confidence from the ground up.

I thought, *I'm not good enough, I'm not beautiful enough, I'm not smart enough*. My learning disabilities had become a constant inner conflict, because I didn't know what was wrong with me. I just couldn't seem to put my finger on it. Everybody said, "You're smart, but you can't do this, you can't do that." I was so limited mentally, and that's very scary because you don't know how to explain it to yourself.

I didn't know I had ADHD and dyslexia back then; nobody really talked about it. It was the beginning of giving kids medication to relax them. I just knew I was disadvantaged, and something was blocked in my mind, so I couldn't do tasks that regular kids did. But I had no clue what I was doing. I tried so hard to succeed in school on my own, but to no avail.

With my dad out of the picture, and my mom too busy caring, working, and providing for us, I had no adult to turn to. I'll never forget the kind Iraqi neighbors who took me in as if I were their own. They let me hang out in their apartment after school, and their kids would help me with my homework and study for exams. They were amazing, and I still appreciate their kindness to this day.

Classical music, opera, old jazz, and blues really influenced me. Old Indian music—especially when women sing in Indian—completely relaxes me, and I still love it today. I've always been drawn to meaningful music. It's the one thing that can shift your entire paradigm in an instant. You can be in the worst mood, put on the right song, and suddenly feel joy. So, of course, music played a huge role in my life—especially since I was also singing. For a short time, I really thought I was going to be a singer. I even did three soundtracks for movies. But in the end, life took me in a completely different direction. Nothing major came from the music, because I realized I wanted to do other things.

I had a teacher who constantly told me I was stupid and that nothing would ever come of me. She'd say, *"You're useless. Nothing's going to come of you, so go make me a coffee."* Every day, I made her coffee. If I couldn't focus or study during class, she'd call me stupid again and send me to make more coffee. And I did. Of course, there was no support. When I told my mom about it, she came to the school once and got mad at the teacher—but within a month, I was back to making coffee again.

My mom just didn't have the time. She was working from nine in the morning until seven or eight at night. It wasn't possible for her to be involved in school. She never came to a single ceremony or school event—not to see me dancing, not to see me singing. I was always the kid on stage, looking out into the crowd and seeing nobody there. I had no support.

That's why I think I became more resilient and strong because I was the only one who had to pat myself on the back and say *you're amazing, you're so good, you're going to make it, don't worry*. It's weird, but I did have these conversations, talking to myself about myself, like a church pep talk. I was afraid of drugs because I visited my father in prison often and heard stories about this guy who became a junkie and this guy who almost died. And drugs really scared the hell out of me. I did smoke pot when I was a kid because somebody gave me some, and it was horrible and weird. I didn't really want to smoke, so it was always in the back of my mind that one day I would quit. And one day, I just made the decision. I said to myself, *You know what? Today, I'm going to smoke a lot, and tomorrow, I'm going to quit.* And that's what I did.

I was always very good at making decisions if something wasn't for me. People offered me cocaine and heroin, and even men who tried to date me said, "Oh, hey, come on, just take a little wine." I realized by their faces and how they spoke that it wasn't something good. They were trying to control me. I'm not a person you can control. I'm very, very strong mentally, and I never got drawn into that. It also scared me to be controlled by something. I always knew that my direction was going to be better, my life was going to be amazing and great, and America was always in the back of my mind.

When I was twelve or fourteen, I was always reading books that educated me. I always sought out really good books and surrounded myself with people who were smarter than me so I could open my mind to different worlds. I met really cool people, like girls from different neighborhoods, and they would take me to live shows and teach me and tell me about their studies. I really wanted to study, but I was afraid. I actually took a course in psychology, but I ended up not completing it.

However, I studied psychology through The Open University (a public research university and the largest university in the United Kingdom by number of students). That really expanded my mind, my thinking, and my ability to absorb things from a medical point of view and how to help people. This changed my perspective when I was studying psychology. I read a lot of criminology books and surrounded myself with books, people, and things that opened my mind to a different world. The idea was that when I did meet criminals, I would be able to look at them like a therapist and not like a person from a family like that.

My dad was released from jail when I was thirteen and decided he wanted nothing to do with that world. He said, "I don't like criminals; I think they're all crazy, and they want to stay stuck in the same paradigm. I don't like that." So my dad opened a legitimate business. He simply didn't want a part of it, and I respected him for that.

The saying "Don't judge a book by its cover" is as real as it gets. Whether someone is an ex-junkie, lawyer, teacher, plumber, or celebrity tells you nothing. Even if somebody has a highly respected job, but is an asshole, there is still a lesson you can learn. You can learn what *not* to be. So, the most important thing is to leave your mind open to learning from people around you and never limit yourself by saying, *Oh, I could never do that,* or *Oh, I could never.* Try to reconnect to that childlike imagination, always leaving a little space for that creativity to thrive, and never limit yourself. Always leave a little portal open. Limiting your thinking is a way of limiting yourself.

All along, things I thought I could never do were just limitations in my mind. And when I opened that portal of not limiting myself, I could start something and finish it without even knowing the full process, but by following guidelines and succeeding. So stop limiting yourself. We have to remember the world is very big. People speak many languages, eat all kinds of food, and have different cultures. So, don't limit yourself to one culture or one habit, like eating the same food all the time.

For example, if you love Indian food, don't eat just Indian food or just Mexican food. You always have to broaden your perspective and mindset to other things because you might like it. It might open you up, it might change your life, and it might take you on different journeys. And that's how we should operate as human beings. And I think that's amazing. To change that mentality from survival to unlimited and creative, you have to understand who you are first of all.

Second, as I said before, open that inner conversation and start asking yourself questions. Keep a little diary or notebook. Write the questions down, sit with them, absorb them, and search for the answers. You'll be surprised by how many insights come to you—answers you never even thought of before.

And don't be intimidated. Don't think, *Oh, she's smart, she's educated, she must have better answers than me.* You'd be surprised how many highly educated people with degrees are actually clueless outside their specific field. They might have technical knowledge, but when it comes to self-awareness, emotional intelligence, or recognizing the beauty and depth in life—they often fall short. They're trained in one narrow subject, and that's it.

When you start expanding your thinking, it becomes easier to try new perspectives and approaches. Take it day by day, step by step. Because when we do that, we begin to understand that life is a long, never-ending journey of learning.

I had a list: every day, I had to learn three new things. It could be anything—sentences, words, a new language, something about the IRS, the government, American culture, or even other cultures. So, set that goal for yourself: three new things a day. If you're learning a new language, start with three new words or three useful sentences.

Every time you learn something new, you open another door. You expand your mind. You stop being limited to one town, one city, one state, or even one country. You become more open to the world—and the world becomes more open to you.

Many people, the majority of people, look at their limitations by comparing themselves to others. When you compare yourself to others, you can never go forward. You can never compare yourself to other people because we are all different for a reason. We have different upbringings, different beliefs, different paths, different goals, and different reasons why we were put on this earth. The only person we should compare ourselves to is ourselves. You don't need to be better than everyone; just be better than you were yesterday.

When I came to America as an immigrant, and I had to do a cleaning job, I didn't say, *no way! I was an actress, everyone knows me.* It only starts from the point of what you can produce at this given moment. This moment in time will take you to the next moment, to the next level, exactly like a never-ending chain of effects. So, if you start with cleaning jobs, you save a little money, and you can open a cleaning company. If you work on your feet, by doing that, you can buy a bicycle, or you can buy a car. These are the circumstances we are given. And when you start comparing yourself to other people and thinking you're not good enough, you can do a nine-to-five job, save a lot of money, and buy property with an FHA loan. For example, in different states, you can get an FHA loan and become a landlord for a four-unit building.

So, it all really depends on how you absorb it. If you think you're going to be a billionaire one day, there are steps you need to take emotionally and mentally to grow because a billionaire doesn't become a billionaire overnight unless you go down that road. You have to first figure out how to do real estate, how to invest, and then you make your first million. And then you think, *I made my first million, so I can make ten million.* Then, when you make ten million and twenty million, it's always like a step and ladder that you have to climb. And when I say ladder, when I talk about that invisible imaginary ladder, I'm not just talking about what you accomplish and get physically. I'm talking about mentally. Our capacity is limited only in our brains. If you cannot imagine making a million dollars in your mind, you cannot make that million dollars in the outside world.

When you can start imagining that you're capable of making a million dollars, you can also begin executing it in the real world. You can save money. You might start with $50,000, use it as a down payment on an apartment, and then, the next month—or the next year—you save again and take out a conventional loan for another apartment or a house.

That's why it's so important to climb that *imaginary* ladder—to stretch your thinking, build your courage, and fuel your enthusiasm. Because if you don't understand that everything works together—physically, emotionally, and mentally—you risk creating illness instead of health.

Everything is always synchronized: the outside world reflects the inner world, and the physical is deeply connected to the emotional. When you align your abilities, your body, and your mindset, it becomes easier to grow, expand, and live in a state of unlimited abundance—always.

You're going to have obstacles, yes, but when you start thinking like that, it's way easier. It's very important to take at least ten minutes every day to sit down with yourself and ask thorough questions. Think and make plans and write down things you want to accomplish. It's very helpful when you write it down, and if you don't accomplish it, ask yourself why. Ask questions, and if you don't know about real estate, start watching YouTube videos. When you're done with YouTube videos, take a webinar. When you're done with the webinar, take a physical course. There are always ways to remove the limitations on yourself and create your own growth because, at the end of the day, we are the best teachers of ourselves.

We are the best at overcoming our own limitations. We are the best psychologists for ourselves if we're not afraid to catch all these things and don't give another person the power to fix them. It's really important to understand that nobody knows you better than you. Nobody loves you and cares for you better than you do.

CHAPTER 4

One of my hands has multiple scars—three injuries on the same hand. One injury happened when I was born. I was premature, in an incubator for a few months, and I was allergic to iodine. I had something on my hand that the doctor put iodine on, and it burned a portion of it. Then, when I was a kid, I had a bike accident and got a scar. Then, during a terror attack, I fell on something hot, like hot plastic, and it burned even more. Nails and glass got into it, too. I often felt like God said, *"You know what? I'm going to challenge you."*

That's how I felt my whole life. I already had a boyfriend when I was a teenager who didn't want to hang out with me because of this scar. It was very, very bad—it gave me horrible, post-traumatic feelings. Every time I talked about it, it took me back to those horrible feelings, like, *why do I have to be such a cripple and deformed?* That's how I felt. And my ex-husband would talk about it all the time. When we wanted to have sex, he'd say, "Oh, put a shirt on, it's disgusting, I can't look at it." It was a complete turnoff for him. And I felt horrible.

This relationship was an abusive one, and one day in particular I'll never forget, physically or emotionally. It was on the eve of Yom Kippur, which is a Jewish holiday, a special day where we pray to God and ask forgiveness for all our sins while in a fasted state, so that meant no driving, eating, or drinking—nothing but straight fasting. Before the holiday, I was driving us when he asked, "When can you transfer money into my bank account?"

To which I responded, "I don't think I'll be doing that."

And his response? Smashing my face on the dashboard because I dared to say no. The entirety of Yom Kippur, we were arguing, and then came the big blow—a hit to my stomach, and I was pregnant with twins. That day, he left a six-month-pregnant woman bleeding, crying, and scared on the floor by herself. I had to walk to my aunt's house, bleeding. It was not far, but her son broke the fast and took me to the hospital. (During Yom Kippur, forbidden actions include driving or biking or anything that exerts physical energy.) They had to put me in emergency surgery and remove a baby from my stomach, which was the twin girl of my son. And imagine all the trauma—sitting in the hospital, crying all by myself with no family, just my twenty-year-old cousin there with me. I didn't know what to do, all I could think about was losing my baby. And then he said, "It's okay, at least we have one left," like it was nothing.

Men don't understand what it's like to carry life inside you and expect twins, and then you're left with one. I felt like something died within me. It was a terrible experience, and in the years after, I suffered so much. That's when I started making the decision, at some point, to leave that toxic relationship because my family didn't protect me from him, and he didn't respect me and treat me with love, was not attracted to me, and was always laughing at me. I decided to leave the country and change my life.

But you have to remember, I was an actress. Although I took a break, I went back to acting after I had my baby. When you go out as an actress to a film festival or whatever it is, everyone is cheering for you, and you remember who the hell you are again. *Oh yeah, that's right! I am an actress, I am talented, I have skills, I have all beautiful things coming for me for a reason.*

Words from my childhood also came back to haunt me, screaming in my head as painful reminders: "You speak too fast." "Oh, you write like an idiot. Like a three-year-old." And I thought, *Yeah, I'm on the cover of a magazine, but the world doesn't know who I am. I have all these limitations in my brain… dyslexia, ADHD, and dyscalculia.*

I know it sounds crazy, but if people talked to me today, they wouldn't believe I ever thought that way. But at the time, that's truly how I felt. I couldn't physically make any changes to my situation yet, since my husband at the time didn't want anything to change. I respected his decision, but in my mind, I was free to contemplate my future to my heart's content.

What my heart truly desired was to be in America. To be a true American. America—a place where people from all over the world came to pursue their dreams, without being defined or limited by where they came from. In my eyes, being an American wouldn't define me; America would finally allow me to define myself.

I started planning: *I need to create a portfolio. I'm a good makeup artist. I want to do eyebrows. I am very good at it, and it's the only thing I can do because I cannot be an actress, as I'm not good enough.* But even when I landed in America (I had an O-1 visa, like an artist visa), I was still afraid to go to auditions. I thought, *They're going to know who I am. This is America. They're going to know that I'm only beautiful with makeup. They're going to know that I'm only beautiful in pictures. I'm not beautiful when I come out of the shower.* I had all these things in my head. I was debating what I could do for work in America, so I applied my skills to my new life in America. I came to an agreement with myself, *Okay, I will stick to cosmetics where no one will see me; I will do eyebrows; I will do makeup.* That's the agreement I made with myself. But honestly, there was one last straw that made me snap and drop everything to move to America.

I always had the will, but I never had the courage until my son's life was threatened, and I snapped. One day, I took my son to school, and there was a terrorist behind us. My son was saying, "Mom, there's a guy with a bloody knife coming toward us." You know, you always hear these horror stories, but you never think it'll happen to *you*. I looked down at my son and smiled, proud of his creative imagination, thinking he was starting a game where we'd run down the street away from the imaginary bad guy.

Unfortunately, ignorance is bliss, and about ten seconds later, I heard a branch snap and a big, heavy, sweaty hand on my shoulder. My heart dropped. My first instinct was to shove my son to the side of the sidewalk and run. The terrorist fell for it and chased me instead of my baby. I understood that, to a man like him, a grown woman had far more to offer than a child. In his eyes, I was prey. I ran and ran until I could no longer catch my breath. I don't know how I ran that much. I knew I was dead either way, no matter how far I ran. My legs only carried me because I knew the farther I ran, the safer my baby would be.

Eventually, I took a sharp turn into a shop and lost the man. The kind shop owners drove me back to my son. As I held him, I called the police, and they took it from there. After that, I finally took him to school and went to work. And that was what it took for me to decide: *I am not staying here.* In a matter of two weeks, I sold everything, gave away everything I had—my high career, everything I had—and came to

America with nothing but $3,000 to my name. And I decided no matter what happened, I was not going back.

I was disappointed that I had been in a toxic relationship with my husband for almost ten years, through my acting career and everything else. I realized my biggest mistake was choosing a man with the same mentality as my parents—he wanted instant gratification and was a bit controlling and narcissistic. And I thought, *I'm stuck in this cycle. I've been in this toxic cycle for years; I have a son, and I have my career, but at home, I'm a completely different person. I'm suffering because I always get degraded. He always puts me down, saying, "You're stupid, you're dumb, even your mom thinks you're dumb. You're illiterate, you can't read or write properly."*

It started eating away at me because I didn't feel like I was maturing—I still felt like a kid, working on autopilot and doing whatever needed to be done out of fear. My parents liked him, and he was cool and good-looking, but I didn't look beyond the surface. I should have been asking: "Is he sensitive, deep, a good provider, a good man, and does he treat me with respect?" I didn't see any of that. I was oblivious to what a healthy relationship required. I was at a disadvantage, as I didn't even know what a healthy relationship looked like.

We only live life forward and understand it backward. Today, looking back, I realize that I was a young kid who knew a lot but didn't know anything when it came to heavily considering the outcome of our choices. I had never seen a healthy relationship, and so I genuinely believed this was how relationships were meant to be until I discovered the golden key. If I had never seen one, that was fine. I just had to create one. So I looked inside myself and asked, *What would a relationship that makes me happy look like? What would make me feel safe? Feel loved? Confident?* And whatever answer was within me, became my new standard.

Through creating my standards, I learned the art of calculating a person's worth by the values they have. We're all different, with different needs and desires, which is why a decision this important shouldn't be based on someone else's relationship that we've only seen from an outside point of view. Who cares what their relationship looks like if we can't know what happens behind closed doors? All we should care about is what happens behind our own closed doors, and what I wanted to feel behind closed doors was security, respect, and love. Look inside yourself, and be true to yourself, and the golden rule will never fail you.

I felt like I was a nanny to my son. And he would tell my son, "Oh, thank God you didn't turn out looking like your mother. I hope you're going to be tall like me and not tiny like her." I could never say anything. It was really hard for me. I said to him, "You know what? The separation is taking too long. We can't come to an agreement. Everything is about money. Money is a materialistic tool. It's not my soul, it's not my freedom, it's not my happiness. I want to remove that equation where I'm depending on someone financially." He hijacked all the money I had because I was naive, and failed to consider the possible consequences of putting him on my bank account.

When I met him, he didn't have a dime to his name and was headed toward a dark path. I saw it, and I got him out of trouble. I sent him to business courses, I opened a business for him, I bought him two cars, and I paid for everything. He became successful, and I put him on all my bank accounts. And that's it. I got screwed. So, I had to weigh what was more important to me—being with someone in a relationship, in a household where everybody laughed at me and put me down, or going out, being an actress, and having people see me as the human being that I am and not just an object for money, sex, and dishes.

I was raised in a culture where women were taught to love, support, and uplift their man and family. And it's a beautiful mentality if given to the right person. But when all that love and support is placed in the wrong hands, and even toxic and abusive hands, it's taken advantage of. What's more important? Is it my self-respect, self-esteem, and money, or my peace of mind, my soul, and my accomplishments, and, hopefully, in the future, finding a healthy person or even healing myself first before I meet anybody? I realized I was the problem because if I kept picking the same pattern of men over and over again, even though it was only three times, I would have an issue. I had a problem. So, I decided to just let go, and I moved to America.

The day before I flew to America, I contacted my friend's uncle, who owned a rooming house in Florida. He was flying with me to the States, so I asked him, "Hey, can you take my luggage? I'll pay for it to go to America."

And he was like, "Yeah, I can take two suitcases."

When I got to America, he told me he gave one suitcase to his female friend, and they lost it, and he was sorry. I arrived in America with hardly any clothes—just the ones I was wearing and maybe a couple more in a small bag I had. I had no belongings, no blow dryer for my hair, nothing. I also had my son and two thousand dollars. And that's when the real boot camp began. That's when the real struggle began. Even though I had emotional struggles in Israel, I'd rather face the challenge of starting from scratch with people who didn't know me than stay with those who put me down and made me feel unworthy, unattractive, unimportant, dumb, and illiterate. I suffer from Dysgraphia, which is a neurological learning disability that affects my writing abilities, and I had an injury from a terrorist attack, so you can understand that it was really hard for me to function like a regular person.

Remember, I could not write an email; I could barely write. I was illiterate in a way. Even if I wrote a phone number, I always wrote the numbers wrong, so I couldn't follow up with people. I was terrified of technology because of my condition and because of this voice in my head that said: *You cannot do it; you cannot read, you cannot do math, and you cannot write.*

Thankfully, I caught these damaging negative thoughts in time to come to a realization. As an actress or a model, when people tell you that you're beautiful, you get paid for it—it's a business, and it's of value. Although I was just a struggling single mom in her mid-thirties who had come to America, working cleaning jobs, I never let myself forget my value. Sure, I was struggling at the moment, but my situation was only temporary. Everyone starts somewhere, and I knew that after I'd gotten through this little bump in the road, I'd do everything I could to use my value to my advantage.

Everybody told me, "You're so smart. You're so beautiful." Every man on the street tried to get my number. Everywhere I went, I felt I was competing with women. Everywhere I went, guys tried to take me to dinner and stuff, and because I had integrity, I didn't want to go with guys that I didn't know or wasn't personally interested in, to use them for dinner. But I realized very quickly—this was typically considered normal. This was how they did it. Guys, take you to dinner, and you can float from dinner to dinner. And I thought, *You know what? I don't have a lot of money. I didn't have money to buy a lot of food and stuff in the beginning. I'll feed my son with the money I make, and in the evening, I'll go to dinner. I'll go on dates.* But because I felt guilty, horrible, and bad in my heart, I decided, as I sat at that dinner—starving and dying to eat—that I would be super polite, super nice, and listen to the person. Some people are truly looking for serious relationships, so I kept my mind open to turning it into a real, meaningful friendship.

I was terrified of sleeping with men because of the scars on my left hand. I could not get naked. I felt deformed. What people saw on the outside was definitely not what I thought on the inside. Finally being in America and meeting all these new and amazing people helped change my point of view for the better, and broadened my perspective about myself, and people in general.

In my childhood and in my teens, I lived in England on and off because people were looking for my dad, and we had to go there for a while and hide. I was in England and Scotland. I traveled all over Europe in my teens, on and off. We had to keep my location hidden. Life was completely different from traveling in Europe, Thailand, and India. It was completely different because all of a sudden, you had to pay taxes, go to offices, and pay for your medical insurance. I had to learn everything like a baby. I had to start from zero. I had to do everything myself. Even though nobody ever helped me with anything, at least I knew the language perfectly. Even though I knew English very well, it was not my native tongue, like Hebrew and Arabic, which I grew up with. I had to learn and take baby steps. And I loved that, because nobody knew who I was. And I knew when somebody gave me a compliment, it was sincere.

When somebody wanted to take me out to dinner, they really wanted to get to know me. When somebody told me I was talented at doing eyebrows or makeup or whatever it was I did, they didn't know me. They had no ulterior motive to tell me these things. They just said that because they saw a girl doing this, doing that, and they could give her a compliment. And I loved it. I felt like Cinderella. And I didn't need to feed my ego anymore with "Sheena Ray." Even after I started getting more involved with doing celebrity makeup, and mingling, and being on the red carpet, it was natural to me. And people would say, "Oh, you shouldn't be the makeup artist, or the eyebrows, or the hair, or whatever. You should be the star on the red carpet. Look at you, it's so natural. You stand there, and you own the place." I wanted to go back to show business. I just wasn't ready to beg for people to see my potential, and if they didn't hire me, I would feel miserable. I didn't want that. I wanted to stay in control.

When I was fourteen, I made a friend who was a top model. Her name is Nina "Vic" Brosh, and she was the most beautiful woman I had ever seen. She was a top model for years in Vogue. She did campaigns for Chanel, Calvin Klein, Vivienne Westwood, and Jean Paul Gaultier. She was born the same day as me. We kept in touch over the years. She ended up in New York and, at one point, had been homeless, too. We grew up similarly and shared the same traits, and the same attitudes. We could read each other without speaking, finishing each other's sentences. She was gorgeous—stunning.

Over the years, she became a supermodel, retired early, and then lost her husband to cancer. We stayed in touch, and I was often embarrassed to tell her about my situation. I said, "Look, life takes us on different paths, but I want to do things that are meaningful. I don't want to just act or sing for my ego or be a famous makeup artist. I wanted to be a motivational speaker."

She always told me, "You know how to talk. I could take great photos, I could do million-dollar, billion-dollar campaigns, but what do you want to talk about? I'm scared and terrified." She always said, "Oh, I love the confidence you have when you talk. You're not afraid to show your feelings; you're out there."

Coming from her, that gave me a lot of confidence. As she was successful and she was telling me she envied one of my abilities, things started to click in my head. I wasn't there yet. I knew I had the beginning of a good conversation in my head. At times, I would stand in a room by myself, talk out loud so I could hear myself, and write things down so it would really plug into my brain. But I hadn't yet put together the whole idea of being a motivational speaker, and a meditation guru, and someone who writes a book. I was still thinking, *I'm not good enough. I'm not that person. I wish, I wish, I wish.* That was my vocabulary. Every time, I'd say, *Oh, I wish I could be like that.* My thoughts about myself were consistently negative. I didn't have a problem giving other people compliments, but when it came to me, I was never smart enough, I was illiterate, and told myself *I can't do that.* I knew something had to change.

With all that being said, I still listened to lectures. Every night before I fell asleep, I meditated. Even when I repeated negative affirmations to myself, I kept trying. And I kept falling—over and over again—for more than ten years.

I have dyslexia and ADHD, so my mind is a little chaotic. Because of this, I like to make order out of the chaos. I would take my diary, like a notebook, and I would start investigating possibilities. What are the best places for people to go? How can I meet celebrities? If someone mentioned they knew this person or that person, I would keep in touch with them, write their phone number down, write on my calendar what they do, who they know, and how I could collaborate with them.

Slowly, I started going to these places. One day, I realized there was a place on Melrose where the guys sold gowns and costumes for celebrity red carpets and photo shoots. And there were a lot of celebrities coming in and out. I was broke. My phone screen was completely shattered. But I waited for about three hours outside of the store until I recognized Joyce Gerard from the *Housewives of Beverly Hills*. I was always dressed nicely with nice makeup, and I got in there and pretended I was looking at gowns. I said to her, " I saw you on *Housewives of Beverly Hills*. I just came here from Israel last month." Of course, I was lying. "I can't believe I'm seeing you. You're the first celebrity I've seen. You're so amazing. I would love to do your makeup."

She was a little suspicious, but I think my put-together look drew her attention—my makeup, my hair. She told me, "I'm going to give you my assistant's email, and he'll talk to you. With my dyslexia, I didn't know how to send an email. My son was small at the time, and I had no one to help me. It took me about a month to find someone to help me send the email to him: *"Hey, I'm sorry, my name is Sheena Ray. Joyce gave me your email, and I know you're her assistant. I'm sorry I was out of town."*

We connected and began conversing. I told him I'd been an actress in Israel, and I sent him some information. Actually, I found a girl in my building who was helping me. We took screenshots from newspapers I had and some links on the internet. And she sent him a bunch of stuff about me. Finally, when they realized I was legit, Joyce texted me on her phone and said, *"Hey, I have an event. If you want to come to my house, this is the address, and this is the time. But please confirm, if not, I'll bring someone else. There are a lot of people who want this opportunity. If you want to come and do my makeup free of charge so I can try you, then come."*

I was ecstatic, and I borrowed about $300 to buy more foundation, creams, and new stuff so that my kit would look amazing. I went there and even did a live show on Facebook. That newfound connection changed my life.

Now, you have to remember that it was thirteen years ago when nobody really lived on Facebook. And nobody really advertised groups or anything. I think I was among the first to actually do that. And I started doing this live, and the next day, I got tons of messages in my inbox. *"Wow, I would really love for you to do my makeup,"* I was booked for birthdays, weddings, bar mitzvahs, you name it. I started to get a lot of business and thought, *I know I did something right. I knew I had to do this. I knew something would happen. I was just myself.*

I hadn't relied on my mom to give me a job or a director to think I was smart, pretty, or talented enough. I had created something. I created a business of my own. I was finally working, and one day, I realized I had too much work and only two hands. What was I going to do? So, I started hiring people. I put out an ad, *"Looking for a makeup artist, hardworking,"* and I started auditioning makeup artists and hairstylists. I started offering these services to people. And that was my first company.

At first, I didn't set it up as a formal company with proper documentation and IRS registration. Then somebody told me, "You cannot work like this. This is dangerous. You could get in trouble. You have to pay taxes. You have to open a company. You have to do it legit." So, I asked people to teach me how to do business correctly. And I was excited and screaming like a little girl, "I'm a business owner, I'm a business owner, I did it on my own. I'm in America. I have a tax ID. I'm paying my taxes." Oh my God, I was so excited to pay my taxes. You don't understand how excited I was to do something on my own and learn. I was writing down every single thing they taught me and told me, so I wouldn't forget. I would go back to my notes and remember what I needed to do to be successful and grow my money.

And then one day, I thought, *"You know what? A miracle has happened in my life. God, or the universe, or whatever higher power, flipped the coin, and I'm making money."* So I decided I wanted to do something. I told my friend who had a Costco card, "I need you to come with me to the store."

When we went to the store, my son said, "Why do you want to come here, specifically?"

I explained to my son that I had an extra-large shopping list that day. I bought a lot of bread, and buns, and pastrami, and mustard, and mayo, and drinks, and plastic bags, and tampons, and pads, and soap, and I prepared a lot of bags with goodies for the homeless. I got things especially for women because being on the street with no tampons and no hygiene was hard. It really saddened me that so many homeless people didn't even get the essentials. I prepared all these bags, and I said to myself, *Let's start going to places where there are homeless people and start giving away stuff.* It was a little scary because a lot of them didn't understand what we wanted. Some of them asked for money. Some were a bit scary. But we went to these places, and my son said, "Mom, I can't believe people live like this. I thought we were in a bad situation."

And I was like, "Realizing that there's always someone in a worse situation than you is important. That's why I'm always telling you that you have to look at yourself in a better situation and how you build from that situation."

And he said, "Mom, you know what? That makes me feel so good. Please, let's do it again."

And from here, our tradition was created—every time I made a little extra money, we would go and buy stuff. Not expensive, but whatever I could afford. It felt so right to give back to the world. I felt so amazing doing that. And there were no cameras, no TikTok, no Instagram—I didn't do it for attention, likes, or followers. It really made me feel good because I reflected back to when I had nothing to eat, and a guy essentially dropped from heaven like a guardian angel sent to me and generously extended me $10,000. What's more, my name was getting out there, and I was building all these new connections, and I was finally on my way to success, building a successful life out here in America for my son and me. What are the odds? If I'm not giving back, then what am I? Am I learning from what's going on with me in my life?

Also, my Jewish beliefs were always present in the back of my head. One of the core values in Judaism is charity. Judaism holds that every month, ten percent of your income is dedicated to supporting those in need. It's a beautiful concept called *maaser kesafim*, and just like Karma, I believe that what you give is what you get. Not only does it feel like the right thing to do, but when you give, God gives you a hundred times more. I came to the materialistic world to live materially, but I combined it with spirituality. And if I get more material than another person and I'm not sharing some of it, then I don't deserve anything. And that became my guideline, to help as much as I can.

CHAPTER 5

I was successful with this business. Of course, I hadn't become a millionaire yet, but I soon had food on my table, a roof over my head, and a car that I could drive. I even managed to limit some of our other spending even further so I could move my son and me to a better zip code where he could be in a better school district. One day, I went to this Israeli woman's house to do her makeup and her family's makeup. She gave me a check—a very large one at that time, about $2,000. I went home, deposited the check, and it bounced. She told me to deposit it again, but it bounced again. This turned into an eight-month saga where I was chasing her, begging for my money. She kept giving me the runaround, saying yes, no, yes, no. I told her, "Listen, I bought the specific brands and shades you requested, I gave you my time, my crew gave you their time, I paid for the gas to bring us all out to you, I had to pay for their food during the many hours we worked with you, and I already paid them out of my pocket. It's not right; you need to give me my money."

She eventually said, "I'm sorry, but you're not going to get paid."

I was furious and didn't know what to do. Back then, I prioritized my appearance—push-up bras, looking super sexy, and long hair extensions. I looked threatening to a lot of women, especially Israeli women, because of the mentality that if you look good and sexy, you're out to steal their husbands. So, I called the woman's husband, he came, and he gave me the money. She freaked out. She was shocked and asked how her husband gave me the money, especially since I didn't know they were in the middle of fighting and divorcing. She went on Facebook and wrote a whole paragraph accusing me of taking her husband and sleeping with him.

At first, I didn't even pay attention to it. I didn't think it was a big deal because I knew it wasn't true. But I didn't realize that this lady was a friend of my cousin, who had always been jealous of me. My cousin had tried to look like me and talk like me—everything I did, she did after me. My cousin told her, "Nobody likes her in Israel. She only dates married men. She probably tried to take your husband." And that's where the conspiracy theory began.

Soon, the majority of my clients, all from my community, started canceling their appointments. I'm talking about cancellations where I could have made thousands, but instead, I was losing thousands. I found myself with no work, no income, no food on our table, and what was most hurtful was that there was not a soul by my side. After burning through my savings, I resorted to begging. I begged my uncle for a couple of hundred dollars so I could fly my son and me to Miami, where I could distance myself from the negative environment that was taking me back to a place I had spent years trying to get away from. In Miami, I knew people who owned a salon where I had worked before. I called them, and they offered to rent me a section of their salon. It was amazing, and I opened my own place, which was very successful. The people there didn't know about the shaming I had faced, and the crowd there was different, fresh, and welcoming.

The guy who rented a section of his salon to me was sweet, helping me out at a time when I really needed it. I respected him so much for that. That's why I was disappointed when I came across a post on Facebook about that same guy. The nasty post stated that he was a piece of shit, cursing him to die of cancer, with personal pictures of him, including his kids. I remembered what it felt like to be destroyed online, so I couldn't help but respond to the nasty post, saying, "Hey, whatever it is, we're a small community. Please don't write stuff like that on Facebook. It's bad karma. If this is a real issue, it can be dealt with in real life without bringing it online. I know him, he helped me during a really tough time! I just think we should be mindful because posts like these can seriously damage someone."

What I didn't know was that I was messing with a psychopath with a criminal history who was a regular at the police station after being arrested on multiple accounts of harassment and stalking. The man was her current obsession at the time, so standing up for him flipped a switch in her mind. She thought we had something romantic going on, and suddenly, everything shifted. In an instant, I had unintentionally swapped places with the man, and now all eyes were on me. It began ever so slightly. So slightly that, at first, I thought I had just hit a slump of bad luck. But it was just her all along, toying with me until she was ready to reveal herself. The morning after I had replied to the post, I woke up to all four of my tires slashed.

After returning from work, my dog was gone. The thing that made me suspicious was that when I awoke the next day, my dog was back… but not alive. He was dead, and without legs, in a box, on my doorstep. I had forgotten all about the post and didn't even know her name;

meanwhile, it had taken her less than five hours to find out my exact address and begin her tormenting.

I didn't have to wonder who it was for long, because some poor man was paid to beat me to death. He didn't have the heart to, so he was gracious enough to only leave me with a black eye and a broken rib. He felt so bad he returned, begging me for forgiveness, revealing who it was. Infuriated that I was still alive, she revealed herself. With no shame, she would wait outside my house or my business. I think she thrived on the fear I felt. She knew she scared me, and she loved every second of it—I could see it on her smug face. She discovered my history with cosmetic injections and used it to her advantage as she ran to Yelp and Google, posting everywhere she could that I'd destroyed her face.

It destroyed my business all over again. Every morning, like clockwork, I'd wake up to a new hateful post. Each day brought another vile, fabricated story. She paid some people to post them, and others were just mindless followers—like sheep with no brains.

First, I wouldn't touch that sick woman with a ten-foot pole. Second, you could see the damage of years of karma on her face—but take it from me, she didn't even need karma's help with that."

I think the worst part about having a stalker is that there is nowhere to hide. It did not matter if I had run to all four corners of the earth; she would find me. There was no peace. The once peaceful farmer's market was stripped of the positive feelings I had once felt as I was attacked on a fateful Sunday. Within the span of a minute, I got a tap on the shoulder and turned around to see her smug smile, holding a spray bottle filled with acid, headed straight toward my face. God knows how she missed, but she got what she wanted anyway, which was to destroy me from the inside out. It was never enough.

With no time to even grasp that most recent attack, a new one sprung at me, which was another beating that left me unconscious and in the hospital. I don't know if she wanted to kill me, because if she wanted to, she could have gotten a gun and gotten it over within a second. I think she intended to bring me close to death, so close that I would feel the pain but would be forced to continue living in fear, pain, and continuous trauma. In my opinion, this was a fate worse than death itself because, at that point, are you even living, or are you hardly surviving?

As I lay in the hospital recovering, I got the first of many calls from a guy she began paying to call me from a burner phone, saying, "I'm going to rape you, I'm going to kill you, I'm going to kill your little son." The thing was, he'd only call when he had arrived at my destination, so while I lay in that hospital bed and received his call, I could hear the same announcements through the hospital speakers playing back to me from his end of the line. It didn't matter where, whether I was in the market or at a wedding, he always made sure I'd be able to hear that we were in the same location and, sometimes, the same room. I lived under constant threat for a long time. Even now, I've kind of learned how to live with it, but it's still terrifying.

She came to the salon and claimed the alleged stalker was threatening her with a deadly weapon and that I was his assistant. The police came to arrest him, not knowing any better, and put him in handcuffs. She was dangerous, but most definitely not the sharpest, and she had the bright idea to go live on Facebook in the middle of the arrest of the innocent man she had framed. Of course, the sergeant realized what was happening, took the handcuffs off him, and arrested her instead. The police sergeant told me, "Listen, she's never going to leave you alone. She's crazy." As much as I hated hearing these words coming from the only source of protection I thought I might have in this crazy situation, I'm really grateful for this policeman's honesty. His words reminded me how vulnerable I was. No one, not even the people whose only job it is to protect civilians against crazy criminals, was going to help me. This thought was scary, but it encouraged me to move my son to a different zip code in a different school in hopes he would be safer.

To this day, I don't know how, and I don't know what the hell she said, but somehow, she called the school, and they kicked him out the same day. But for this, I'm grateful, too, because it only made me fight for my son's protection even more. It was a dark time because it wasn't only her; she had gotten a massive cult of online haters against me, and these women began attempting to blackmail me. I did my best to hide my son's existence from the online world, but before I knew it, women were threatening me with the one I love most. They'd call me from blocked numbers so that I would have no record of their threats as proof, and they'd taunt me by saying they'd frame my son for hurting their children and pets. I couldn't let this happen; my son was so young and innocent. They didn't care and framed him for stealing and viciously killing two puppies. Once it got to the police, they knocked on our door, requesting my son for questioning. They took him in and took his fingerprints and mugshots as he cried. Of course, he was proven innocent, but this haunted him for years. Because of this, he had difficulty keeping and making friends, and trusting others, even me, and to this day, he refuses to have a presence on any form of social media.

People on the street would ask me, "What did you do to her? Why is she doing this to you?" I would tell them I did nothing, but they would insist that I must have done something. They'd go on to say, "Why would a person do this otherwise?" and I started to question if they were right.

She posted every morning, putting my photos all over social media, calling me a scam artist, saying I ran away from L.A., that the police and the FBI wanted me, that I stole money from old people, and that I slept with married men.

What's crazy is that she was racist, and people still sided with her. She created a story about how I pretended I was Israeli so that I could get close to Israelis and screw them over because, apparently, I was secretly a Jew-hating Muslim with Black ancestry. Unfortunately, people believed this story because she knew exactly how to blend the truth with the lies, all to make it appear that much more believable. It was true that some of my grandparents were Black, and some of my grandparents were Arabic, and I was not ashamed of that and would shout it from the rooftops! But what she did was take my DNA and turn it into a shameful story of lies.

My name started to get really big, but not for good reasons. Imagine waking up in the morning to your name being slandered. People started assuming things about me just based on the way I looked—sexy, with fake boobs. Immediately, they assumed I was a bitch, a whore, or all these other horrible things.

So, basically, she destroyed my life. And with that being said, the other girl from Facebook, who posted that big paragraph, said I left L.A. because I slept with her husband. She destroyed my life, too. Now it was two people collaborating against me, both of whom were very strong. It was non-stop harassment. Every single day, people would stalk me, blame me, talk badly about me, and threaten me. I was terrified. I saw people waiting outside my house.

When I opened that business, at the same time, I met a guy who became my fiancé for two years. I went to Israel to visit my family and stay away for a while. When I got back, I found out he had stolen my social security number, bought Rolexes in my name, and only introduced more problems into my life while I already had enough on my plate, dealing with a stalker who threatened my life. All these things terrified me.

One day, I was working on a client, and I collapsed. That's when the saga started. I went to the hospital almost every day—back and forth. They kept telling me I had anxiety, but I knew it wasn't just anxiety. Eventually, I developed kidney problems and ulcers in my stomach, and I was fainting regularly. It took about a year and a half before the doctors admitted me to check my heart and found out I had a heart issue from all the stress. I got out of the hospital, but they didn't put me on a monitor. Then, I had a minor heart attack, which led to them admitting me again and finally giving me proper treatment. But I had stopped working and had no money. A year later, I became completely homeless.

I had no place to live. A friend and her husband let me and my son stay with them, but we were sleeping in the living room. One night, she woke me up and said, "Listen, my husband and I were talking about you. We want you to leave."

They kicked me and my son out at 1:00 a.m. We ended up sleeping at a Denny's, since it was a twenty-four-hour restaurant. Simple necessities like showering and eating were a struggle, and I couldn't stand to see my son hungry anymore, so I started going to food banks, churches, and even turned to the Jewish community to try to get us help. A few Jews tried helping, but believe it or not, the people who seriously helped me through this tough situation were Christians from the church ,and a Palestinian friend I had met.

One day, I found myself sitting in my car with a flat tire. I had no place to go, and no one to turn to. A message suddenly appeared on my phone. It was from a friend from L.A. He'd sent me a message on

Instagram saying, *"Wow, you live in Miami now. You must be living the good life, probably going to the beach every day."* I told him to call me, and when he did, I was honest. I told him I wasn't living the good life—my son and I were living in my car. I sent him a photo of all the stuff in the backseat, clearly showing we were sleeping in the car. He said, *"Why don't you drive here? In return, you can take care of my pets."* I was hesitant at first because I had a lease on a Toyota and didn't want to leave my car behind, but he helped me get a place.

I was super sick, so I took up my friend's offer to drive to California. But I was so sick that I could barely drive, so my son, who was only fourteen and a half, had to drive. He was scared, but I told him he had to do it. I quickly taught him how to drive, even though it sounds crazy, and he drove most of the way from Florida to California.

A week after arriving in California, I collapsed on the floor and was taken to the emergency room. They told me my heart was in bad condition, my stomach was in bad condition, and I had silicone leaking from my breast implants that was poisoning me. They said if I didn't fix everything, I would die within six months. They also thought I had cancer in my stomach. I was terrified.

I was too embarrassed to call my parents and tell them what was happening. The whole situation sounded too delusional to be real. I sat in the room thinking, *I've lost my clients, my health, my friends, my business—everything. What do I do next?* The first thing I decided was to focus on fixing my health. I followed all the doctor's instructions, took my medication, and thank God, in California, they gave me free medical insurance. I was able to heal and get better. I was scared for my life. But there was light at the end of the tunnel. When I started walking again, even though I was still weak, I decided I wanted to start working again.

I had done facial injections in the past, on and off, without charging people. It was just for fun because I loved it, but I never really charged for it. I decided to take some courses to get better. I met a Russian lady who told me, "You're so talented, I want you to be my assistant." I became her assistant, going from place to place and learning a lot. But I wanted to improve even more, so I took courses in Turkey and Texas. I met a Palestinian girl named Sahar in Riverside, who was amazing. We spoke a little in Arabic, a little in English. Her family came to live in America, and she had become a successful nurse. We became friends, and she sent me tons of makeup jobs. I knew it was taboo because, in both Palestinian and Israeli societies, you're not really supposed to be friendly with someone from the other side. But she treated me like her little sister, taking care of me from afar, making sure I had jobs, talking about me, and posting about me on social media.

I couldn't believe it because, in the eyes of others, I was Israeli, and yet she was helping me. Meanwhile, I had called all my Israeli friends, and none of them wanted to help, except for three people. One was my friend, Oli, from New York, who deposited money for me a few times. Another was a girl named Alona, who gave me $1,000 on one of the holidays. A religious guy and his wife let me stay in one of the rooms they were renting for a few days. It was amazing.

But despite all the new opportunities in my life, I was still haunted by the psychopath every day. I was isolating myself in Riverside, not thinking about any religion, just taking any help I could and making myself better. One day, I was in the hospital, and I decided to read Tehillim, a Jewish book of Psalms. I was thinking, *God, I don't believe in you, but if you do exist, I really need you to show me.* And within a minute, a Jewish doctor came into the room and said, "Hey, are you speaking

Hebrew? What are the odds? I'm Jewish, too. What are you doing here?" I was in shock. That was my sign, and it really opened my mind to see things differently.

I decided to dedicate the next year and a half to resetting my mind and changing it for the better—to throwing all the past away, and becoming a different person. Every day, I would watch videos about how to take out a mortgage, how to save money, how to deal with money—analyzing and learning everything. Even with all my fears, I studied how to buy a house, how to rent RVs, and how to make money from RVs. I got into mobile homes. I learned everything in that field—anything related to having a place to stay. I started working and traveling, getting a lot of clients. My health was still not one hundred percent, but I was okay enough to be mobile.

I decided I was going to buy a house. I tried to get a mortgage in Vegas, but it failed. A woman told me I could never get a mortgage in L.A. because it was too expensive. She said I needed to move to Vegas, where houses were cheaper. I moved to Vegas, but it didn't feel like it was my home. I didn't feel like it was a part of me or somewhere I wanted to live. I got clients, but I had no license there, and I felt horrible. So, I went back to L.A. and decided to change my approach. I looked at it as a pyramid and wrote down what was missing in my plan to buy a house. I realized I wasn't doing my taxes correctly. I was making money, but I wasn't putting it into the business like I should have. I needed to open a freelance business, so that's what I did. I took on side jobs, reported more freelance work on my taxes, and made the necessary changes. When I went to take out a mortgage, I was approved.

The woman handling my mortgage told me it would take two months to move into the house, but I didn't have that kind of time. My lease was about to end, and I didn't have the money to keep paying rent and buy a house. I told her I was going to meditate and move into the house within a week or two. She thought it was nonsense, but two days later, she called me and said, "Honey, I don't know how you did it, but next week you can move into the house." And I moved in.

Everything started improving from there, but the harassment from the psychopath didn't stop. After I moved into my own house, I found out she had paid more than fifty people around the world to open fake accounts to post made-up, malicious gossip about me. I started getting text messages from people showing screenshots of her paying them to do this. But I wasn't afraid anymore. I posted on Facebook asking for help from anyone who had been hurt by her. Despite having a restraining order against her for five years from Florida, she continued to harass me.

After that post, a lot of people reached out, telling me how she had ruined their lives, too. She had closed businesses, accused people of molesting children, and terrorized many others. A whole community was terrified of this one married woman with two kids who looked normal on Facebook but was actually a witch from hell. I was going crazy, thinking, *My whole life, I've been through hell—with my dad and my mom, raising a child, losing my acting career, moving to America to build a new life, and now a person from my community is terrorizing me.*

I couldn't wrap my head around the fact that my own community was against me while non-Jewish people were the ones helping me. I went to multiple rabbis, but they all told me to tolerate it and not post on social media. But my business was on social media—I couldn't just stop. I couldn't understand why my community was abandoning me while others were helping. I knew I couldn't hate my community or my God, but I needed to find a solution to change the paradigm. If I could manifest a house, I could find a way to deal with this situation. But I was embarrassed to tell my story because it was so unbelievable. My friends even said that if they didn't know me, they'd think I was messed up.

When the pain was too much, it was a mental battle. Sometimes, I didn't want to be here anymore. I just couldn't take the harassment anymore. But I thought of everything I had survived and decided I wasn't going to let this destroy me. The only thing keeping me here was the future. I couldn't believe I had gone through my struggles for nothing. Something good had to come from it. That's when I decided my future on this earth would be dedicated to helping others as a result of my experiences and everything I'd been through, so that I could give hope to others who were surviving similar situations. I realized that if I gave in to all the obstacles life threw at me, I would never learn anything or achieve anything. I studied successful people who had been through similar hardships and realized that if they could make it, so could I.

I started building myself up again, slowly but surely. I began speaking in places for free, doing podcasts, and creating something out of nothing. One day, I was at the airport and met Dr. Joe Dispenza. I told him how his teachings had changed my life, how I had bought a house because of him. We had a long conversation, and I realized that anything was possible if you thought outside the box, and stayed in a paradigm of creation.

CHAPTER 6

I tried to reorganize my thoughts. And when I say my thoughts, I don't just mean my thoughts but also the situation I was in, what I had, and how I could create something from it, even if it was super small. I thought, *Okay, I'm sleeping in my car. I have $800 to my name that I'm holding onto tightly, so I don't spend it. And I'm with a little child.* I made a list of people I thought might help me. I wrote the same message to all of them, about six or seven people. I figured if just one person responded, it would be a huge step forward. I wrote, *"Hey, you know me, I would never write a message like this, but I'm in a really bad situation. I'm embarrassed to tell people, and I really need help. I have no place to sleep and no money in my pocket. If you can help me in any way, I would appreciate it."*

Three people blocked me, and three said they were sorry, but were in a bad situation themselves. But one friend, who I hadn't seen in about fifteen years, from New York, said, *"Okay, I'm sending you $350."*

Then I continued thinking. If I couldn't rent an apartment because my credit was really bad and I didn't have a deposit or anything, what should I do? I started making phone calls to people I knew who had more than two bedrooms and a spare room, or to friends who might know someone. I looked for people who needed someone to live in their house in exchange for some kind of help. I found a place where I worked in return for a place to sleep, but when I wasn't working, I spent every moment researching and learning.

I saved like $20,000. But you have to understand, when I say "saved," I mean buying the cheapest food imaginable, like tuna in a can, beans in a can, eggs, and anything I could make at home. I learned how to make potato cakes and other things that could last for the next day as a snack or something. I maximized the food I had and counted every penny. I got to the point where I learned to live on almost nothing. Even when I started having money, I was still afraid to spend it. Looking back, it was evident how badly I was struggling with money anxiety. It can be difficult to allow yourself to feel safe around money, because of the fear that it'll be stripped from you once you feel safe and comfortable again, and then you'll be back to square one with nothing.

Then I learned to buy a house. I saved $20,000 and realized I wouldn't be able to buy a house in L.A. because it's so expensive, but I could buy a house in other states for $10,000 or $20,000. So, I drove to Vegas and applied for loans there. The money was enough, but I didn't realize how much knowledge I still lacked in the loan department. I had spent so much time learning about taxes that I had completely overlooked learning about loans. So, for the next six months, I applied for FHA loans and, unknowingly, did it all wrong.

During that time, I was watching videos, writing notes, and keeping a notebook filled with notes. I was constantly asking people for advice. Then I realized that when I went to the mortgage broker and said I wanted to apply for a loan, he didn't guide me. He processed the application, and when it didn't qualify, he simply said, "No, you can't qualify," and that was it. He didn't sit with me to explain what was wrong. So, I thought,

Okay, if I did one, two, three, four, five things wrong, let's figure out what they were and fix them. I started building a sort of pyramid, figuring out how to apply, identifying what was missing, and taking notes on everything. Whenever something was missing, I replaced it.

Then I thought, *If I can do a mortgage with an FHA loan at this price, it means that if I wait three or four months and save more money, I could apply in L.A.* At that time, I was living in an apartment building and realized that if I took out a mortgage, I would have to skip paying my last month of rent. I didn't want to do that because I had never done it before. I don't like owing people money. But I had to do it. So, I applied for the mortgage, got accepted, and with the little money I had, I put it toward the closing costs and paying any debt. I didn't want to have any debt, especially since I wanted to keep buying more houses now that I knew how.

So, I learned that the first thing you do when you start from absolutely nothing and begin earning a salary is to eliminate your debt. First, you clean your debts, especially if they are not a good debts, and I'll explain why. Second, you clean your credit—no bad history, no bounced checks. You want to have debt when it's a mortgage, or when it's building something, or a liability that eventually pays for itself. At least, if it's a liability that's not weighing you down. For example, you don't take on liabilities like rent or debts that you owe someone for something if it doesn't yield a return. But you do take on the liability of a mortgage that basically pays for itself.

What I did was buy a house with a huge one-bedroom loft in the backyard. The loft could bring in $2,500 a month or $2,000 a month, depending on the tenants I found. This income allowed me to pay the mortgage just like I was paying rent, but in the end, this house would be mine. I wouldn't be paying rent; these would be my walls once the debts were paid off.

Then I realized that after you finish an FHA loan, you can take a conventional loan, or there's a law that allows you to take another FHA loan, depending on your situation. So, I got into all the details with a government loan and then bought a secondhand RV. I realized I had a lot of space in my backyard, so I renovated the RV, hooked it up to water, sewer, and electricity, and made it amazing. I started doing Airbnb from the RV, then earned money from the guest house, and saved up for another mortgage. Renting out all three properties covered my mortgage and left me with $8,000 to $10,000 in my pocket every month, which I could use to take out another mortgage.

That's when I realized there are so many opportunities if you just open your mind and expand it. It doesn't matter if you're a single mom, half-literate, or have complications. You just need to see the bigger picture, take notes, and not be afraid to take action.

When you're in a really bad situation, what's the worst that can happen? You could lose it all, get into more debt, and your credit might worsen, but at least you're trying—creating something out of nothing, creating from the unknown. When you create from the unknown with good intentions, something will happen. But when you're afraid to create from the unknown and say, "I don't have money, and I'm scared, so what am I going to do? I'm going to lose what little I have." That's when you get stuck forever because you're trapped in the same loop of fear. You keep going around in circles, being afraid to put your thoughts together to try to create something. When you get stuck in that paradigm of fear in your creation, nothing good is going to happen.

Remember, you're in America; there are grants, loans, and opportunities. I realized and learned that if you open a company, even if you're starting with little, it's going to cost you some money. And when I say a company, I mean a corporation. A corporation is a big umbrella—you can do multiple businesses under it. In America, every six months, three months, or every year, they offer grants, loans, and SBA loans you can take. It could be a personal or business loan to recover from a disaster. So, you're investing now for a bigger return in the future.

I don't mind living in my RV and renting out all the properties I have if I know that in six months, I'll have enough money to buy another big house—a five-bedroom mansion, or a seven-bedroom house where I can Airbnb it and make a lot of money from it. It's a never-ending story when you take the right loans. At least the money is rolling in, even if you're a little stressed. You can also find a good laundromat or small business that others overlook and create something from that. I had a small business of home services with makeup artists traveling everywhere. Now, I do it better because I know how to make it bring in money in a certain way.

When you expand your mind and are not afraid to try, you can make so much money from things that others aren't even thinking about. In L.A., I realized it's very easy to go to red-carpet events and meet celebrities. If I start with nothing, all I have is my perception, my mouth, and my talent. One day, I got lucky enough to stand on a red carpet and saw Eva from *America's Next Top Model* and *The Real Housewives of Atlanta*. I jumped on the red carpet with my product in hand and let her hold it. I told one of the photographers I knew—because I had gotten friendly with a lot of paparazzi photographers, giving them gifts for their wives and such—to please do me a favor and take as many videos and photos as possible in the few minutes I had with her on the red carpet. He took a bunch of videos and photos, and I edited one video so well that, the next day, I put it all over Facebook. I didn't write that she was buying my products. I said, *"Hey, do you want to have an amazing eyebrow gel that all the celebrities are wearing right now? It's super trendy. I have it at a really affordable price, and you can DM me on Facebook, and I'll send it to you."*

The next day, I got hundreds of DMs from people in Dubai, India, and countries outside of America and Canada. They all wanted my eyebrow gel. The following week, Eva's publicist was telling me they were going to sue me.

"You did a product displacement. You're using this." And I said, "Well, listen, you could sue me, but I don't have any money. I live in my car. My bank account is empty, so you can sue me. I don't know if you'll get the money, but if you have the funds to file that lawsuit, which costs like $1,000 or $1,500, go ahead." So, obviously, they didn't sue me because I knew what to say. But she had agreed to take the video with me, so they couldn't take it down, and I had to use it. I was like an animal, biting and clawing just to get my products out there, and my product became really successful. I spent all day shipping orders. I had a story on Facebook, and I had hundreds of videos on YouTube and Facebook showing celebrities on the red carpet with my product. Every day, I would drop by the red carpet events with celebrities and just let them hold my product, and people assumed that all these celebrities were using my product. It was amazing. I started making a lot of money—I think I saved like $50,000. Back then, it felt like millions to me; this was nine years ago.

Then, one day, this Israeli girl called me and said, "Hey, I love your products. You're so amazing, and I heard you do eyebrows. I'm coming to get my eyebrows done, and I want to talk to you." So she came over, and while I did her eyebrows, she said, "You're working out of this one-bedroom apartment with all the products in your living room. Why don't I invest in your business? I have a big house in Beverly Hills. I'm married to an older guy, and we could make more products."

I said, "Okay," and we entered into a partnership.

She said, "I'm going to put some money in, change the product, and we'll revamp the style, packaging, everything."

Now, remember, during all this time, I had accumulated a lot of debt. Before I learned what to do, I had a previous business selling dresses. I kept trying, and trying to be successful, but I ended up with all these debts, including hospital bills, apartment bills, and collections, so I started paying off those debts. Our business was going well, but then she realized I wasn't very tech-savvy. I didn't know how to manage the website, check things online, and do all that. She opened the bank account and the company—all in her name. Basically, she hijacked my business by being smart about it. Technically, the word is "manipulative," but I gotta give her credit… it was smart. It didn't even take much for her to do it. I was just dumb, to be honest.

So, I ended up with multiple businesses that completely fell apart, losing money. My high-end gowns and dresses business failed, the makeup brand collapsed, the makeup services were gone, and my salon/school shut down. Four businesses had all gone. It was devastating for me, trying so many times, thinking I was doing something right, but every time, I realized I didn't know how to run my business properly. I didn't know how to manage my money and use it to make more money. I wasn't spending on expensive bags or crazy things that many women do. I just didn't know how to save that money, invest it, and do good things with it. That really devastated me, hurt me, and made me feel bad. But still, it didn't click. I didn't realize I needed to learn something. I knew I had a problem, but I didn't go and search for the solution.

The biggest problem we have in achieving success is that many people just don't have someone to give them the right advice. That's the major issue. Most people around us will always lead us to where they are, or more accurately, to the limitations they have in visualizing a bigger picture, or a bigger vision. So, most people stick to safe, nine-to-five jobs. Most people want to do the same thing because they have bills, kids, and responsibilities. The majority won't know how to break it down for you.

I realized and learned in my life that we are the best advocates for ourselves. You don't need to attend an expensive university. You don't need to be born into a rich family; you don't need any of that. You need to listen to your gut, sit down, and take notes. Shut your mouth and listen to people. Elevate yourself by being with people who are more successful than you. You meet one successful person, ask them questions, and take notes. Then you move on to the next one, and the next one.

I realized that even the rich people I associated with were not at a high enough level. I needed to be with those on the next level, the billionaires. That's what I'm doing now. I have an event I'm attending where there are billionaires around. I'm still clueless about that, but there's always a higher level you can learn from. You don't surround yourself with a couple of successful people and think, *Oh, that's it.* You always climb the ladder to higher and higher levels because staying in your comfort zone and just learning from one or two people is not enough.

For every person who climbs the ladder and becomes really successful financially, it's not just luck. Of course, some people have luck, but I realize it's a state of mind, a way of thinking, behavior, and routine. It's what they do, because most of the successful people aren't just successful with money and trips and all that. The truly successful people are also successful in taking care of their health. The most successful people don't flaunt it; they don't show up at parties or flash their wealth. The real successful people are the silent ones you don't see wearing brands. These are the people you want to learn from.

You really need to surround yourself with better and smarter people and not be afraid. I always ask questions like a little kid, and people look at me, surprised. I ask about words I don't know, like "What is utilized?" or "What is this?" or "What does this course cover?" and I write it all down. Because when you hang out with successful people, you want to speak on the same level. You don't want to appear like you don't know anything. Of course, they're going to respect it if you ask questions, but you want to level up your language. You want to level up how you treat your body and how you see things—not just talking, not just being the best in the groups you're in. You want to listen and absorb, just like a scientist who tries to make it work, and if it doesn't work, they try the next thing.

This brings us to the point of changing your self-consciousness, because if you want to change the paradigm and the hard drive you are operating from, you need to change yourself in order to become the person you want to be. For example, if you want to be Bill Gates, you need to absorb how Bill Gates acts and become Bill Gates. That's the only way to do it. Be happy about other people's success. Don't look at it from a miserable point of view, like, *Oh, she made it, she has a better house, she has a better car, she has better, better, better.* You want to look at it through a different lens.

You don't want to see things the way poor people do. I learned how to identify poor people—not exactly poor, but unsuccessful people. That's the right word. Unsuccessful people will always steer the situation and conversation toward something chaotic or tragic. Successful people always finish with a note of success, a higher vision, hope, and hopeful results. They always find a solution rather than focusing on why something cannot work.

When I was in a chaotic place in the beginning, I always found a reason why things couldn't work for me. I always found reasons it couldn't work—because I didn't have money, because I slept in my car, because I had nothing. But there are so many people in America with empty houses, older and lonely people who are looking for someone to live with them, someone to protect their home, or things like that. So, literally, there's always something you can create from—much more than that.

Most of the time, we are oblivious to the opportunities around us, and we push ourselves into worse situations because we're so scared to try to dare to think. Because, at the end of the day, everything starts in our minds.

Every creation starts in our minds, and our minds can lead us to chaos. If you want your mind to lead you to success, you need to expand your way of thinking. When you have nothing to trade with—no nice clothes, no money to invest, no assets to show—it can be challenging in conversations. For example, I would sit in a place where people would say, "Oh, I bought this, I bought that," and I had nothing. I was sleeping in my friend's house, taking care of his dogs. Naturally, this can give you low self-esteem at the beginning of such conversations. But, of course, there's the saying, "Fake it till you make it." I'm not suggesting you lie like crazy, but you can strategically shape perceptions.

One way to do this is by talking up a previous business or project to create the impression that it was instrumental in your current success. For example, you might say, "One of my previous mobile services companies was a great foundation for what I'm doing now." This positions your past experience as a valuable stepping stone without overstating it. You can talk about things you've done in the past, but I recommend not talking too much at first. Just ask questions and take notes.

Also, examine your inner circle because it can bring you a lot of success. For instance, if you have a mother who saved money, she could lend you some. Or if you know someone—like a girl I met who was an expert at getting loans, like SBA loans or whatever—you might be able to get some help. I also met another person who was very good at helping people get money during COVID. It's important to surround yourself with a variety of people with all kinds of talents, because talents are not always displayed on the surface, like singing or dancing.

A lot of people get excited about superficial talents. I don't get excited about someone who can sing or dance because that talent isn't going to improve who I am as a person. Sure, it's nice to enjoy, but it won't help me grow. You need to look for extra talents—people who know how to get loans, repair credit, secure mortgages, or teach you about currencies.

You have to understand that even people who work at banks don't always know how to use their talents because they're often boxed in by routine. It's important to work in tune with opportunity, with yourself, and with a list of what you need to learn. Always expand the way you look at other people. Observe successful people, see what they do, and learn from them. Don't be afraid to take ideas and look closely at your surroundings.

Your close circle can always offer something. Maybe you have a family member who can let you stay rent-free for three months in exchange for some help. Or perhaps your close circle can lend you money or offer you a temporary job. Many people want to be millionaires, but they don't want to take a less glamorous job for a while just to get by, and instead, let pride get in the way. You can't operate if you don't have something in your pocket. So, even if you take a job at McDonald's, save money, and then buy your first property in Atlanta, whatever it is, because you live in America, you can take out a mortgage wherever you want—there's always an opportunity.

The thing is, the majority of people are lazy, and the most dangerous people I've encountered are the lazy, ambitious ones. If you're ambitious and lazy, you become miserable when others succeed because you can't do the work, get your hands dirty, and start from nothing. So, before anything, you need to figure out who you are. If you're lazy, you have to motivate yourself because nothing is going to happen otherwise.

How many homeless people or prostitutes do you see on the street? And I'll explain why I see homeless people and prostitutes in the same equation. Many prostitutes, and I mean it in a broad sense—it could be any type of prostitution, high-level or not—are women who are too lazy to work and use their minds to make money. They want an easy way out. They don't think about the long run or consider the consequences of their actions. So yes, they might make a lot of money from OnlyFans now, but what happens when they're in their forties, fifties, or sixties, with kids, emotionally drained, and considering suicide because they've tainted their family's name and can't take back what they've done?

So, that's the thing. If you want to be lazy, if you want to align yourself with lazy people, you always have to question yourself. Or do you want to be with the people who actually dared to get up, even when it was hard, rainy, cold, or hot, and just do things? You see, a lot of homelessness because it doesn't matter if you're a junkie or an alcoholic—these people have a void to fill, often stemming from unresolved emotional childhood trauma. Instead of getting up and overcoming this trauma, they live with it every day, polluting themselves with drugs and other substances instead of building something out of it.

I don't care what you've been through in your life; it's never an excuse to lie down and be on the street or do nothing. I'm not saying it couldn't happen—I've been on the street myself, so I know it can happen—but it needs to be a very temporary situation. The most time you should spend on the street is three months. Then, you need to get a job and start building a foundation for security. That's the maximum time I would allow someone to be in that situation.

But you must work through it. You can't be on the street and not work through it. You can't just wait for a miracle or for someone to drop $10,000 from the sky and say, "Hey, I'm the knight in shining armor. I've come to save you." Many people, especially women, think that way. Women often believe they'll meet a rich guy who will take care of them and their children. I've heard hundreds of women say that. They really believe these fairy tales, but it's not going to happen. Nobody is going to save you unless you're really lucky. And even then, I don't see it as luck, because if it's handed to you, you're most likely going to lose it.

So, the first thing is to realize that you're alone in this world. It's only you and God, that's it. If you have more than that—like family support—then you're really lucky. But for most people, we are all alone. We need to sit with ourselves, see what we have, and work from there to make our way in the world.

I personally never drink, never smoke, and never do drugs because it's very easy to go down the wrong path with those habits. For me, it's really important to always stay on the right track, and remain focused all the time. I can be at the best party where everyone is going crazy, but I'm always thinking about business 24/7. I'm constantly considering how I can meet the right people. I look for big events where I know there will be billionaires, speakers, and people who can elevate me.

In L.A., you can meet someone who can elevate you anywhere, even if they don't intend to. Even if it's a groupie girl with a lot of connections, she can still provide you with valuable connections. But you need to know how to select and differentiate: this one isn't good for me, this one is okay just to hang out with, this one can introduce me to important people. Everyone has something you could use. And when I say "use," I don't mean to use and abuse—I mean that you always need to have something to exchange with them, something to bring to the table.

For example, I have various abilities: I can do makeup, eyebrows, injections—I can do a lot of things. So, when someone helps me with something, I might take care of their Botox or fillers for their wives. I had this girl who was super rich, living in the Hidden Hills, but she lost a lot of money and was in a bad situation. I told her, "I'm not going to charge you anything; just give me access to certain people, give me information, introduce me to the right connections." She agreed, and I got a lot of business through her. She brought me top-notch clients, for instance. Another person might get me into specific places. So, anyone can elevate you; you never know in what way.

Chapter 7

In any industry, I believe it's the same thing: Never give up. Please stay determined. Always look for opportunities. Don't tell yourself, *Oh, I finished working at five o'clock, and I'm not taking phone calls anymore.* You have to be on the clock 24/7 if you want to be successful. No matter what, don't be like those people who say, "Oh, I'm sorry, I finished working; these are not my hours." You don't want to be like them because they miss opportunities, and you don't ever want to miss out. Be willing to change your calendar and schedule at any moment. See the opportunity in everything. Don't be afraid to jump on a flight, if necessary, to take a specific course that will elevate you to the next level. You have to be willing to do almost anything, of course, except sex, drugs, and things like that.

Because you could be in a situation where you have nothing, but when you have nothing, you actually have something. I know someone who started as a driver and worked his way up. Although he's not a millionaire, he's still successful—he's made good money and invested in real estate. So there's always something you can bring to the table. As long as you have yourself, your health, and a good state of mind, there's always something you can build from. The majority of humanity can't entirely grasp the full potential of their abilities until they've experienced life at its lowest point. If you really take the time to truly understand yourself and your talents—study yourself inside out, make a list of your strengths and weaknesses, a list of people who can help elevate you, and opportunities you can explore—you will discover that you are much tougher than you could have ever imagined. Most people just act and react from the automatic pilot part of themselves, essentially just going with the flow instead of taking the opportunity to wake up, explore their surroundings, make a plan, and execute it from there. It will only benefit you. It might take longer, or it might happen quickly, but there's always something you can bring to the table. You just need to be willing to open your mind and not listen to those people who say, "Oh, you have no money; you can't do it." Come on, man, it's not impossible. I've been homeless, and people didn't give me the time of day. Even my son thought I was delusional when I was homeless. But then, when I bought my first house and put money aside, he was shocked. He was like, "How the hell did you do it?" So there's always a way. We just need to realize that we can either choose to look at the opportunities or choose to focus on the bad situation we're in. It all begins and ends with your inner conversation and your ability to see the end goal. You need to act and think a bit like a crazy person. Believe in the impossible. It's not impossible.

It's really hard to see the impossible when you have nothing. Often, when we have nothing, our brain allows us to make excuses. But we have to remember that these excuses are only keeping us at the bottom. Do you think people at the top got there by making excuses? Hell no. If we wanna get to the top, we gotta act like the top. It's crazy to think about now, but even when I had nothing, I hustled, and every extra penny from every hustle I was doing was invested in my mind. I spent hundreds of hours working to spend hundreds of dollars on courses, materials, tutoring, and anything else that I needed to give me the information I needed to succeed.

At the time, I didn't have enough to invest in houses, but it was one of the greatest investments I ever made for myself. I say it's crazy because if you saw someone sleeping in their car and found out that they were paying hundreds of dollars for a course, you would look at them and want to scream, "Are you crazy? Go buy some new clothes that aren't torn, or start saving for rent. What are you doing?!" I wasn't thinking of what I needed at the moment. I was thinking about the bigger picture. I was thinking about my future. I knew that when the time came, and I got my opportunity to elevate myself, I needed to be prepared. I needed my brain and all the things that I had learned to help me stay at the top and continue elevating myself.

That was my starting point, and it was scary at the time, but it was worth every ounce of fear. Most people don't see the end goal. And if they see it, they often choose to ignore it and make excuses for not daring to believe in the end goal. They don't see the end vision. They don't have that perspective. With me, I don't know how I saw it, which is crazy. Sometimes I can't even believe it myself. For example, in the last week, I've been seeing myself living in a mansion with twenty rooms, twenty-five bathrooms, and all that, in my dream city in the perfect area. The only thing I see in my mind is this. This is, literally, the only thing I visualize all the time: *When am I moving to this house?* A house there starts at five million. I don't have five million yet, but I'm not just looking for ways to get there—I'm aiming to think only of the end goal.

Because the universe, as crazy as it sounds, will eventually take you there. The universe will find ways that you won't even imagine. That's happening right now as we speak. I opened in a field that was a treasure trove of opportunities because the makeup business taught me a lot, especially about the importance of advertising.

You cannot save money on your advertisement. It's essential to keep a notebook or some form of a list of your clients and maintain regular contact with them. My makeup business taught me that you have to work on your products and many other little things, but mainly, you must keep in touch with your clients. They are the ones who can go to Yelp, Google, Facebook, and Instagram to give you reviews. They are the ones running your business behind the scenes because they tell other people and do a lot of the networking for you. That's really important.

For me, working in the makeup business was about understanding the financial progression. When you don't have money or are used to working in a profession where, for example, you make $30 from eyebrows on each client and then $200 or $170 from makeup, you start to see the value differently.

When you elevate yourself from making $30 to $200 per person, it feels like a lot because you still have that worker's mindset. It took me ages to elevate myself from being a worker to someone who could sit at home and make money from something like Airbnb. It was really scary because I had to let go of the thought that I needed to make that $30 or $200. It took me ages to let go of my makeup business because I felt like I was losing a job. I had made a lot of money from it, but it was nothing compared to the injection business.

Then, when I moved to injections, it was hard to let go of that, too, because I thought, *I'm not going to do injections anymore because I have to focus on Airbnb now.* But Airbnb gave me a lot more money without the stress of trading my valuable hours for money. That became my end goal: to focus on Airbnb and real estate. When you leave a service profession, you don't have to deal with people the way you do in one-on-one services. You deal with people differently, with more power and less need for explanations.

As you become elevated in the world of making money, it's not just about having more money in the bank; it's about not wasting your time and energy on things that don't bring you that same energy in return. It's draining to get caught up in the small details, like being late, grumpy clients, manipulative clients, or clients who are always asking for discounts. When you deal with small service businesses, you often deal with people of low to medium-low incomes and a poor mentality. As you continue to elevate and make more money, you start dealing with people who are more financially comfortable. They don't nitpick every penny. They have also elevated themselves, so your energy changes, and you're no longer dealing with a poor mentality.

This should be your end goal: When you make money, you don't stop at the first or second or third business, until you reach a point where you don't have to deal with anything anymore. People handle it for you, and everything operates automatically. That's the end goal. I didn't know this; nobody taught me. Nobody told me, "Oh, you don't want to deal with these people." It kind of happened naturally, and I realized, *I can't believe this, I don't have to hustle for $30, $200, or $300 anymore.* Now, I can work for six months and peacefully maintain the business for the remainder of the year. But even then, I realized you can't afford to rest until you have $20 million in the bank.

You can consider exiting when you have $20 million; it's okay because you'll be good depending on your age, goals, and whether you want to travel or do other things. But if you want to continue, you always keep going because the more money you have, the more businesses you can create.

The more money you have, the more freedom you have. If you're smart and pay attention to the small details, you can either become a billionaire with lots of liabilities and headaches from continuing to build small businesses, or you can create businesses that give you less headache. It's not just about having money; a lot of people without money look at rich people and think, *he's rich, he's got a lot of money, and that's all there is to it.* But that's not true. There are many rich people who are locked in their own mindsets—rich people with a poor mentality who keep working like slaves. The whole point of having money isn't just to have money. At the end of the day, it's materialistic. But behind the materialism is the true reason people want to have money: freedom, peace of mind, a sense of security, and time. Time to enjoy yourself, enjoy your spouse, your kids, your parents, and all your loved ones. And finally, now that you are elevated, you can elevate your loved ones for generations to come.

I can give you a good example with my mom. My dad came from a rich family, but my mom came from a poor one. She became a millionaire from nothing. It wasn't quick—it took years—but when it happened, it happened quickly. Despite her wealth, my mom always had a poor mentality. When she had her business, she would jump from task to task, working physically and even saving money by doing her cleaning herself instead of hiring someone. I used to see her making 200,000 shekels a month and still cleaning her own business. She wouldn't let go. She interfered so much in her business that people got tired and didn't want to work for her anymore, because she was driving them nuts. She never realized that time is money.

So, a lot of rich people, especially the newly rich, remain locked in a poor mentality. I've seen many who lost their wealth because their mindset prevented them from moving forward. It's crucial when you make money to match your energy and state of mind to the level of wealth you've achieved.

Today, there are many motivational speakers in the market, especially with short videos on YouTube, Instagram, and TikTok. People look at these quick videos and seek instant gratification. Most of them don't even attend workshops, webinars, or seminars; they just watch these short videos. Many entrepreneurs in these lectures say things like, "You don't need to save money; saving money is stupid," or "You have to buy real estate," while others say, "No, don't buy real estate." There's a lot of black-and-white advice based on their personal experiences.

The first thing is to take everybody's advice, but always look at it as part of a bigger picture—a net or umbrella under which there are many approaches. But you need to remember, if you didn't come from money, you can't just expect things to happen because you manifested it; you have to put in the work.

Even though I went to multimillion-dollar networking events at night, dressed beautifully, met celebrities, and offered them my products, I was cleaning Airbnb houses during the day. I preferred cleaning Airbnb houses over working at Starbucks or something similar because when I cleaned, nobody saw me. I would clean the Airbnb house, leave, and have money to keep things rolling. If you don't have a cash flow, or if it's not a lot, you can't keep going. You need to be willing to climb the ladder and take any job necessary. You can't just decide, *I'm going to be a high-level person,* and expect it to happen without putting in the work.

I'm not going to interact with these small people. I'm not going to do this. I'm not going to do that. It's not going to happen. I met a lot of women in L.A. who revealed how they refused to do their own dishes, laundry, and cook for themselves and their families even though they could not afford to hire a cleaner or go out to eat every night. These women did not prioritize their financial goals, as they were too busy prioritizing their egos. A lot of people didn't see reality as it was, refusing to look at themselves and their financial situation for what it truly was. It was almost like they were blind from denial, living in a lie. The problem with their denial was that without acceptance, they could not grow. They never allowed themselves to admit they were poor, and the consequence was that this never gave them the opportunity to use their financial situation as motivation to grow out of it and move on to bigger and better things and places.

I've seen it happen many times, when these women go from rich guy to rich guy, going out to five-star restaurants every other night, getting gifts, and even going into a bit of debt to afford something expensive for themselves so that they can play into their fantasy. But when the fantasy is over, they go back to their one-bedroom apartments and say good night to their roommate. Unfortunately, these women got so comfortable playing pretend that they basically just forgot it's not their life, and they are just a temporary side character in that fantasy. You have to be willing to do anything because, even if you have money, things like COVID can happen and hit everybody. Nobody expected it. You always need to be prepared, 24/7, for unexpected scenarios and be willing to take any job that comes your way if something happens.

I did a lot of things to get started with Airbnb. I would go to people's homes and do their blowouts and eyebrows. I would go into salons, and because I didn't have money most of the time to pay for a room to do eyebrows, permanent makeup, or whatever it was, I offered them forty percent and told them I would sit there until I got work. I had about three salons that I would hustle at, two or three times a week. I'd ask if I could talk to the clients, and I would bring my iPad and prepare pictures ahead of time. I'd say, "Hey, how are you? My name is Sheena Reynolds. I'm new here. I'm offering amazing services. If you want to do your eyebrows or makeup, I'll do it for the first time for free, and you can recommend me to your friends and give me a shout-out on Instagram."

I would literally give them my services for free the first time, in exchange for a review on Instagram. These reviews brought me a lot of clients because people would see the posts on Instagram or Facebook, and reach out to compliment my work, and want to book an eyebrow or makeup appointment as soon as possible. Especially if I saw celebrities, I would offer them multiple services, since they go out a lot. I went to the homes of many celebrities, like Barbie Blanc from the TV show *WAGS*. I would do her makeup for free and do a live video on Facebook or Instagram. I always looked for ways to bring in other people. If I was doing all this for free, I made sure I was getting free advertising and marketing in return, to utilize them to bring me tons of work.

People who are locked in their minds could never be successful unless they got lucky. I've never met anyone who was a long-term successful person who wasn't willing to do the work. Only lazy people sit there and say, *What am I, a slave for hire? What am I going to do, work for other people? Work for minimum wage? With an ugly uniform, just like everyone else?* I've had friends who said this, and I was genuinely astounded at how many people lived their whole lives in that box, proudly judging others. I knew an acquaintance who became a millionaire. She met a guy who was a millionaire and had many homes, rentals, and Airbnb properties. She stuck to him like glue, offering to drive him, do things for him, even get him girls. He got used to her doing everything for him—messages, emails, taking him places. Today, she has about twenty Airbnb rentals.

It's really about what you're willing to do to reach your end goal. Some girls do it with OnlyFans, some by sleeping with men. That's not my way—I'd never do it, but it's about what you can tolerate. When you do business, remember, if I were to be on OnlyFans, I always think about what would happen if I became really successful and wanted to go into politics or start a huge company and be the CEO. How could I sit at the table with all these people if they could just scroll and see my private stuff? So, I'm always thinking about outcomes. It's very important to consider the outcomes of the dirty jobs you're willing to do. Every action has a consequence, and the consequences can be good or bad; it's up to you. You're the author of your own story. You're the director of your own movie. You are the main character. So, what kind of main character do you want to be? How do you want your story to end?

But you always have to set your ego aside when it comes to deciding what jobs you won't do. Also, believe it or not, I've saved a lot of money by not smoking, drinking, or spending money on my nails or hair. Think about it: if someone is willing to spend $200 every two weeks on their nails, that's about $4,000 a year. You could save a few thousand dollars every year, which you could use to elevate yourself to the next level.

Chapter 8

I knew I needed to change. Sometimes I was really clueless about what to do or how to wrap my head around making the right decisions. I did a lot of business and made a lot of bad decisions. It was only when I started asking myself questions like, *How come I make a lot of money but never know how to keep it?* or *How come I make a lot of money but don't know how to invest it?* that I began to see the issue. My conversation with money was always along the lines of, *Money is important, but I don't care about it. Forget the money.* For me, it was all about doing the art, doing the eyebrows and makeup, and that's a really backward mentality. You really jeopardize yourself when your attitude toward money is, *I hate money. I don't like money. Money is the root of all my problems. I don't need money; I just do it for my art.* The majority of people look down on others who value money and view them as greedy, vain, and shallow, but that kind of thinking isn't accurate. It's backward. In this materialistic world, money is the key to moving around, the key to freedom.

It's really bad, because if you don't know how to manage yourself, you can't manage your business. I'm the business—not just my skills, not just my talent. Wherever I go, I create from the unknown, from nothing. So, if I treat money like it's not important, it becomes a problem. You have to understand it goes even deeper than that. We live in a very materialistic, physical world, but we are very spiritual creatures. We base everything on intuition, on how we feel. You can meet someone at a big event, and they could seem amazing to you, but as soon as you talk to them, you feel no energy with them, no connection. So, no matter how you approach it or how much money you make, everything is based on energy, on inner conversation, on spirituality in a way.

It doesn't matter what the situation or end goal is; you need to build relationships, have chemistry, and do the right things to get the right results. You can't just go on with bad energy and expect good things to happen. I really needed to change, but I didn't fix it in one day. It took me years because I always meditated and did various things, but I was often clueless, working on autopilot. I didn't know how to aim for what I wanted. I didn't know how to set specific goals and ask the right questions. When you look at the world as a genie, where you just ask and shall receive, things start to change and elevate very quickly. It's hard to tell yourself that because you think, *I swear, this is like something from the movies; what am I, a five-year-old, thinking like that?* But yes, this is part of it. Part of it is manifesting in a way where you're not afraid to go all the way in your thoughts, to think like a crazy person in order to bring something from the unknown, from the unexpected.

You have to sit and make lists all the time. Remove negative people. Have end goals. Don't be afraid to approach high-level people and start a conversation. You can fake it till you make it a little, and that's okay as long as you're not a compulsive liar. Utilize your money with priorities—figure out what the priorities are with the little you have. Don't be afraid to think outside the box because everything starts within us. Even a chair in your dining room started as someone's thought until it was manifested, built, or designed. Everything starts inside us. The key to this physical world is knowing how to manifest it from your spirituality, your thoughts, and your insides, to the outside world. And that's the secret. That's the secret that nobody talks about. Most people know what needs to be done—you need to work, study, whatever it is. We know what needs to be done. But most of us don't know how to manifest it—how to bring it into action, depending on what you're doing. Being honest with yourself is very hard because we don't want to admit things to ourselves.

I saw this lady who was living with me in this shabby apartment building. One day, she was working in the salon doing lashes when Kylie Jenner ran away from the paparazzi and hid in her room. She quickly thought on her feet and started taking a bunch of pictures with Kylie in the room. The next day, this girl posted all the pictures and became a millionaire from her lash business. So, I'm trying to say that you need to think quickly and jump on opportunities when they come your way, especially if they come spontaneously. And don't be afraid to dare to do things that others might find embarrassing. Some might say, " I was too embarrassed to take a picture with her. I didn't even do her lashes!" But that's the moment that will build you—the moment you actually dare and are not afraid to do things, even if the outcome isn't what you expected. Because only when you dare to do the unexpected do opportunities come your way.

I think most people stand in their own way. Why do you think there's a herd mentality in this world? Most of the world follows the herd, and there's a reason for that: Most people cannot step out of themselves and their egos to do what it takes to go low to rise high. Most people are afraid to even think about it. One might think, *I'm not going to skip my yearly vacation.* A lot of middle-class people can never give up their annual vacation. A lot of women say, "If my husband doesn't take me on vacation this year, I'll get mad at him." A lot of men could be more successful if their women were willing to adapt to living less comfortably for a couple of years, maybe three years. So, a lot of people stay stuck in that middle ground because they cannot step away from all those little luxuries they're used to—like having a cleaning lady, going on vacation, buying jet skis, buying luxury toys, spoiling their kids, and spoiling themselves.

It starts with the little things. When you eliminate the little things you think you need, that's when you become stronger because you realize you don't have to live large or spend a lot to be successful. People, especially women, often jeopardize themselves because many women have big egos and are not willing to compromise. They don't want to let go of treating themselves or dating someone who is in the same place as them, but also trying to elevate themselves. A lot of women want to marry a rich person, a millionaire, or a billionaire immediately, and I think that's wrong in a lot of ways. You want to be with someone you build that wealth with, because then it's equal. No one can come and say, "When I met you, I had no money. I took you for nothing. Look at you now, living like a queen," and then she's scared to get a divorce because she's afraid she won't live in the same world anymore.

A lot of women, with their mindset, jeopardize everything. Women need to be more restrained than men because men don't have a problem putting on gloves and doing the dirty work. For women, it's a problem because they don't want to give up their small luxury assets. Like I said, the highlights, the injections, the vacations, the birthday parties, the extravagant nonsense like Valentine's Day, birthdays, Fourth of July—all this nonsense. Women have a lot of issues with this. The women who don't usually have these issues are the ones who don't look so good and who don't really invest in themselves. It's really hard to find that middle ground. If you're a woman who loves how you look and invests in your appearance, usually, you don't invest in other things.

Of course, I'm generalizing right now, but that's usually what happens—not a lot of time and effort is put into building a really successful business. It's either you're very successful in business but don't look so good, or you're very good-looking but not investing much in an industry like permanent makeup, nails, injectors, where appearance matters. I mean, today, things are changing a lot, I'll be honest, I think men are more willing to give up their luxuries to climb the ladder, while for women, it takes a harder hit or jealousy to motivate them. Jealousy can drive people to do crazy things. It really depends on what kind of ego you have. If your ego is fueled by jealousy, it can give you a lot of drive in a good way. If your ego is driven by people telling you, "Oh, you could never make it," that's my kind of ego. So, it brings you to the point where you need to know what kind of ego you're building from, because we all build from our egos. If you have an ego that drives you to win no matter what, or if you're jealous of your friends and want to be like them, that's one type of ego. If you have an ego that just doesn't exist, if that makes sense, you break it down into these little pieces, and there's always something that motivates you, something that could carry you to the next level.

Or you see homeless people on the street who have just given up. I know people who were millionaires, but during COVID, they lost their money, moved to an RV, and just gave up. They don't want to be part of this matrix, fighting and working hard. They say, *I have my RV, I have a little job, and this is a bucket bed. I don't care. I have a roof. I have food. I don't want to do this anymore. I did it for so many years.* I know a lot of people who find comfort in their daily habits. They go to church, they have a little job, they have a little apartment, and they don't care anymore. Many people don't want to be stuck in this cycle. They make millions and then just retire and live their lives quietly. So, there are many ways to escape from the matrix—it depends on how you look at it. It can be a mindset. It can be spiritual; it can be financial, all of those things, but it's internal, not external, because the external doesn't mean anything.

Let me give you an example of the difference between Middle Eastern and American mentalities. An American person might say, *I'm eighteen or twenty-something, I'm not going to live with my parents, absolutely not!! It's awkward, it's embarrassing… no way.* They leave their parents, rent their own apartment, and try to build from there, but it's more difficult. Then you see Middle Eastern people saying, *Why would I go live outside when I can live with my parents? We provide together, save together, save more money, cook together, clean together, do everything together, and then I elevate myself.* So, it also depends on who is surrounding you. If you're surrounded by people who left their family home early, disconnected from the family, and think they have their own show to move on, that shapes you differently.

Family wealth starts with how you view and treat your family and your surroundings. If you want to build family wealth, you can't be one of those people who say, *Oh, I don't live here anymore. I'm eighteen, so fuck my parents. I'll visit them twice a year, whatever.* That's how they're going to grow old with their money. They'll grow old, their kids will put them in a nursing home, or they'll grow old with no kids and just some pets. The family's wealth stops there.

Look at all the billionaires with old money—they're always taking care of their families. It starts with how they have their own bank, which is the trust fund, and how they utilize money through life insurance. They even have their own life insurance debt. Just like having a life insurance policy, this serves as collateral—something you base your loans on. You loan money to yourself, invest in yourself, and build your own wealth.

Now, the people who think like that usually become rich for generations. The people who neglect their parents and the people who tell their kids, "Oh, fuck off, you're eighteen," don't make that "fuck you" money. If you want to make that "fuck you" money, where you have endless freedom, you need to bring the close people in your life to work with you. For example, your sister could be your personal assistant. Your parents could help you by taking out a loan from the bank. Your mom can cook for you. Your dad can work for you. You bring all the people into your business, so when you grow, they grow with you.

The people who think, *Oh, I'm going to do it on my own, fuck my mom, fuck my dad, I don't need them, they're older,* are thinking stupidly. If they don't know how to think and utilize money, you need to teach them, just like they taught you their values. You need to be there for them, just like they were there for you when you had nothing. It's a back-and-forth, psychologically healthy game that you play with your family and surroundings.

The people who don't have this healthy back-and-forth with their surroundings are the ones who are going to lose their money, do drugs, or end up as millionaires doing cocaine on a boat with ten girls. These are the people no one talks about. I've never even seen a self-help book mention this because most people don't have this deep understanding of real money.

Take, for example, the Hilton family. When Paris Hilton went down the spiral, lost things, made mistakes, did drugs, and partied every night, she always had a healthy foundation behind her. That foundation let her do her own thing, but when she needed help and reached out, it was there for her, and she bounced back. The same goes for Kim Kardashian, the Trumps, and anyone with generational wealth. The people who don't elevate back, who don't grow back, are the ones who don't take care of what's close to them and where they come from.

You can't come from a mother's womb and say, "Fuck my mother." The core values of who you are will keep you moving upward. You can climb up the ladder to the top, but God can also drop you down fast and hard, or it could take forty years. I met a guy two weeks ago who grew up in a trust fund family. He lived off the trust all his life. But when he was sixty-five years old, his dad died, and his mom decided to cut him off. Now, he lives like he's poor; he doesn't know how to survive. He was about to commit suicide because he didn't know how to survive.

So, you could have that "fuck you" money, but if you don't have the skills and morals, it will catch up with you one day. Your inner conversation and your morals, when you make money, will ultimately dictate your future when you're eighty years old—whether you'll be in a nursing home where someone can use and abuse you or you'll grow old in your family's care with all the luxury. The relationship you have with your family, whether you've been nasty and mean to them or kind and good, is the point.

All the memories I have of my mom from when I was a little kid, a teenager, and even in my thirties are kind of fading away today because she has become a completely different person. It's not the person I remember—not just physically because she's aged, but also mentally.

As a mom myself, I'm kind of scared that my son will one day see me in a certain way—a negative way—and just feel sorry for me when I get older. So, I find myself stepping on eggshells with how I speak to him, how I raise him, and how I make decisions as a mother. I'm constantly questioning myself. It's really hard because I'm always torn between raising him out of guilt and correction, or being tough and consistent. I worry about whether he'll resent or hate me for being strict.

When I was a child, my mom was super tough and strict. Everything had to be exactly how she wanted. I didn't like it. But as I grew up, I realized that her approach made me resilient and stronger.

The whole point of my book is to open and expand the reader's mind—to show that it doesn't matter where we come from or how we grow up. There's always going to be an outcome, a conclusion, because it's all part of a learning process. At the end of the day, some people go on autopilot, doing things without questioning them, even when they're harmful. They don't realize that every action we take impacts the next generation. After we're gone, our behaviors, attitudes, and parenting choices will carry on.

I believe that, as human beings, many of us don't use all the tools and abilities we were born with. When we parent, build relationships, or pursue careers, we often operate on autopilot based on how we were raised or what we saw growing up. We don't always realize that we can choose to be different or better than what we've known.

Only when we push our limits, question ourselves, and dare to explore new perspectives can we truly grow. Opening our minds to other cultures, languages, and ways of life doesn't mean we have to change who we are, but it helps us understand others and become better, stronger individuals. We don't have to stick to the automatic behaviors we inherited from our families.

Life is short, and as someone who has experienced a clinical death, I know that consciousness doesn't just disappear—it continues even beyond physical existence. That's why it's so important to keep questioning, learning, and evolving. We owe it to ourselves to live in peace with who we are, both now and for eternity.

When I became a mom, I often found myself hating parts of my own behavior. I would catch glimpses of my mom in me—getting mad at my son or trying to parent him the way she did. Suddenly, I understood why my mom acted the way she did when I was stubborn or defiant. It's a harsh realization because, as much as I disliked her strictness back then, I now see myself doing the same things.

Everything we do in life, whether good or bad, comes back around—not as karma, but as lessons that repeat until we learn from them. If we reject one lesson, it reappears in different forms until we finally face it.

When I think about my mom, I often try to see her from an outside perspective—not as my mom but as a person. This helps me understand her and learn from her choices. Becoming better means not being afraid to act from a place of growth and change. But it's tough because each situation feels like a test.

When faced with these tests, I ask myself: How should I act? How do I want to be as a mom and as a person? Sometimes it feels like the universe or God is giving me the same scenario repeatedly, but now I'm in my mom's role. I'm the mom now—not the daughter. Life has a way of swapping our positions to teach us something new.

CHAPTER 9

Shifting from a survival mindset to a growth mindset is something I have tried to do for years, even though I didn't realize I was trying. I didn't have that conversation with myself. It starts with a conversation, as I said before. I didn't have the conversation to shift it because even though I saw my mom struggling—even as a millionaire—she was always in survival mode. I knew it was wrong, but I just didn't know how to explain it to my son. I didn't know how to say, " I don't want to be like my mom, always in survival mode." I just resented her for being in survival mode.

When I became very sick, sitting at home, unable to function, and weighing only thirty-four kilos with no money, no connections, and no clients, I started having these conversations with myself about survival. How did I get to that point at forty years old, homeless, living in someone's house, feeling annoyed and dictated to, and being driven nuts because they counted how much food I ate from their pantry? I would steal rice and other things because I didn't have money, just to survive. I was renting rooms from him when he wasn't home. I had to steal rice, pasta, and eggs to cook quickly before he came back, and even some vegetables. It was a very low position to be in.

I got to the point where I taught my son how to steal food from the supermarket. It really made me feel terrible about the values I was passing on to him—that we were stealing food just to survive. But you have to understand that my son was a teenager and physically small, like me. When he was fourteen, he looked like he was ten. When he was eighteen, he looked like he was sixteen. He didn't develop into a big man, and I was scared for him. What was I passing on to him?

Even though I told him, "Listen, Sean, I'm not a thief. You know me, your mom, you know my values, but we don't have food. It's going to be easier for me to steal with you." I taught him how to manipulate and play dumb when we were stealing food in case we got caught. And I hated myself for that for years. But as he grew up, my son was so smart. He came to me and said, "Mom, I remember how you told me it's wrong to steal unless we have to survive. And you taught me how to do it."

My son appreciates food so much now. He cooks really good food. When he goes grocery shopping, he tells everyone, "This is not healthy; this is expensive." He reads labels, checks prices, and looks for better deals. He's only twenty-one, remember. He would never waste money on shoes or clothes. Last week, he bought Nikes and spent months searching online for a better deal. Instead of paying $130, he paid $65 because he waited for the right deal. I don't see many twenty-one-year-olds doing that; they don't care about saving money or finding a deal.

I also instilled in him the importance of not getting tattoos. I told him, "When you're a big CEO in a company, you don't want to regret having marks from every phase of your life. You don't want to say, 'Oh, this tattoo was from when I was twenty-one, this one from when I was thirty.' You don't want to look at yourself at sixty and see all the episodes of your life displayed on your body. You're not a billboard. You need to get down to business and be serious. In your brain, you can store memories like drawers that you can open and say, 'Oh, this was the time we stole food, but I learned a lesson,' or, 'This was the time my mom taught me how to make bread from nothing.'"

So, I instilled these values in him. I'm not saying it's bad if people choose to get tattoos—that's their own thing if they like it. But I wanted my son to be someone who could blend in, someone who wouldn't stand out if he ever wanted to go off the grid. I taught him real survival skills, not just how to follow trends or fashion. You don't want to be one of those people who just looks like everyone else. If you want to be part of the crowd, that's fine, but I'm not part of the crowd. It was always very important to me to teach him not to be part of the matrix.

So, what would you say to someone who realizes they need to start making a shift? They need to start changing internally. When I was very sick in bed, I realized how much I was just surviving. I got to the point where I had to steal food, and I decided I didn't want to be in survival mode anymore. I wanted to be the kind of person who has savings to rely on, someone who isn't dependent on charity, and someone who is living, not just surviving. When people help you, they often make you feel like they're doing you a favor, and that puts you in a vulnerable position.

There's a Jewish prayer you're supposed to say on every holiday and every time you wake up. It's also supported by science and logic. It says, "God, please always place me on the giving side, not the receiving side." As long as you can give, you're on God's side. I always said that prayer but never fully understood it until I realized that to get out of survival mode, you first have to put your ego aside.

Switching from "survival mode to "boss" mode means becoming someone who isn't afraid to take risks, make decisions, and seize opportunities. For example, I have a friend who came to this country as a teenager. She was alone and had no money. But worked hard and every single month, she bought a few houses and built her business from nothing because she was willing to work hard—working in malls, going from place to place, observing her bosses, learning how they made money, and then copying that pattern to start her own business. She started with skincare kiosks, then opened her own stores, bought real estate, and collected rent. She shifted from being an employee to owning her own business.

I think some people, like Israelis, do this naturally. The majority of Israelis I see in America, and Jews in general, tend to become wealthy despite starting with nothing. I believe some of the credit goes to the hustle mentality in our culture, but what's beautiful is that Jews tend to hustle together. They work within their community, making their family and friends their business partners and employees. This alone shows the importance of connecting with others and networking with others as one of the major keys to personal elevation. Take, for example, the Jews who came to America after World War II, having lost everything. They were often rejected by the established institutions—they couldn't get jobs as doctors in American hospitals or open bank accounts. So, what did they do? They opened their own hospitals, like Cedars-Sinai, and provided work for Jewish doctors. They started their own banks, trusts, and corporations. They found a way around the obstacles. No excuses.

It's all about adapting, learning, and being willing to take the necessary steps to move forward.

I'm not going to mention names, but there are a lot of community complaints, and I want to address the issue of common antisemitic stereotypes, which is important for people to understand. Judaism, in general, is often associated with making money, utilizing money, and making donations, and I'll explain why. This isn't about religion, but rather a matter of fact. Judaism is a religion deeply intertwined with concepts of science, money, and success. Literally, every prayer and every holiday has some connection to these ideas.

For example, the first Jewish holiday of the year is Rosh Hashanah. Rosh Hashanah is a holiday that teaches you how to maintain family wealth. One tradition is eating the head of a fish to remind yourself to always be a leader, not a follower. They teach that wealth isn't just in your pocket or in the bank—it's in your skills and knowledge. You could survive something as devastating as the Holocaust, see your entire family die, and still come to America and rebuild. A good example of this is the story of Marshalls, the retail store. Marshalls was built by two Jewish men who approached the owner when it was a small business and offered to work in the basement. The principle here is that you always have to offer something rather than just *taking*.

Most people have a mindset about how others can help them. However, truly wealthy people who come from generations of wealth—and people who are on the right path, in the right mindset, and just truly destined to be wealthy—are always looking for ways to contribute in return by always bringing something to the table. The founders of Marshalls did just that. Today, Marshalls is a multi-billion-dollar publicly traded company. This is just one of many examples.

I grew up with this mentality of utilizing everything. You don't need to explain this to an Israeli or a Jew; they just understand. We naturally operate with a generational wealth mindset. If you go to any Jewish or Israeli household, everyone helps their family and brings business to their family. The entire Jewish community operates with this mindset of building generational wealth. This is something that families like the

Rothschilds or the Rockefellers embody, but it's actually the mentality of every Jew in the world. We work for our family, regardless of how difficult they may be. They are your mother, your family. You keep the family's issues within the family—you don't air your dirty laundry in public. Whatever problems arise, you solve them together as a family.

This brings us to the topic of generational wealth, which starts within the family. It's about how you support and uplift your family. Everything starts with that foundation. In Jewish families, holidays are centered around this idea. Conversations often revolve around helping one another: "Did you help your brother? Did you open a new business? Your brother needs money—why did you let him borrow from the bank? Why did you move out of the family home when you could have saved money by staying longer?" These are typical conversations in a Jewish household.

In contrast, in other communities, I see a tendency to undermine and hurt each other rather than support one another, and I think that's wrong. If you want to build generational wealth, it starts with keeping everything within the family—money, support, everything. Jewish people don't abandon their family members as they age. They rotate responsibilities, like caring for a grandmother. They ensure that someone is always there to help, whether it's giving her a massage, singing songs to her, or just being present. These might seem trivial to some, but they are crucial to maintaining the strength and unity of the family.

My mother had a poor mentality, and my dad had a rich mentality, like in *Rich Dad, Poor Dad,* one of my favorite books. I realized that I had seen this dynamic in my own household, and I had to navigate between the two. That made me realize that maybe I was absorbing the wrong influences. My dad was sometimes weak compared to my mom, and he was scared to tell her things. I thought to myself, *I don't want to be like my mom, but I don't want to be like my dad either, because he's afraid of her.* So, I realized I needed a new role model. I needed to look for new people who could set a better example. I decided to step up the ladder in terms of who I was being inspired by. I started seeking out and learning from better influences. I looked at different families and cultures, like the Persian and Iraqi Jews, who are very good at generational wealth.

When I looked at Americans with generational wealth, I noticed families like the Trumps. For example, Donald Trump always said, "Give me only a million dollars." To poor people, that sounds like a lot, but when you're dealing with billions, a million dollars isn't much to start with. Remember, you're not competing with poor people—you're competing with billionaires. If you're a Trump and your father had millions of dollars and only gave you a million to start, that amount won't get you far without the right skills and knowledge.

Donald Trump lost billions of dollars and then made it back because of the generational wealth skills he learned at home. If you don't learn these things at home, there's almost no way you'll pick them up unless you're like me and go deep into it. You have to be a deep thinker to really understand these concepts.

I'm not a person of strict rituals, though I have some simple ones. For example, I meditate almost every day because it's important for me to focus, and I nourish my body with healthy food. No matter how many cosmetic treatments and procedures we have available to us today, nourishing our bodies with the right oils, fruits, vegetables, meats, vitamins, minerals, knowledge, and, most of all, a nourishing mindset that provides us room to grow is non-negotiable. I never compromise or save money when it comes to my health and my mental health. I make sure to get regular check-ups and take care of myself internally.

When it comes to my mental health, I try not to waste time on superficial things. For instance, instead of watching something fake on Netflix, I could watch a good lecture or listen to a speaker who could elevate me to the next level. I try to avoid nourishing my mind with superficial nonsense or conversations. When I'm alone, I focus on using my time to advance myself.

Before bed, I'm very conscious of my subconscious. I used to love watching investigative shows and thrillers, but now I avoid going to sleep with images of death, murder, or negativity in my mind. Instead, I listen to high-frequency music that can change my mindset and open paradigms in my brain. I nourish my brain with this music every day before bed. I also spend at least an hour a day on manifestation and self-conversation, focusing on my goals and growth.

I was having a self-conversation about doing something different with Airbnb. Then, yesterday, I had a client who's an expert in that area. She's become a multimillionaire through various apps, techniques, and ways that she rents out her apartments, RVs, and other properties. She started talking to me, and I was amazed. She said, "I want to help you. I want to teach you because you're so amazing, and you've helped me with my faith." So, literally, everything I'm manifesting is coming my way. There's no way I'll manifest something, and it won't happen. The only obstacle when you manifest is how far you can take your thoughts. If you have only a million dollars and want to make a billion, it's a long journey. If you have a thousand dollars and want to make a billion, it's even longer. So, your brain may struggle to even imagine it.

Our imagination can be very blocked when we're in a limited mindset. You have to unlock that mindset. If you can't imagine a million dollars, you certainly won't make a million dollars. If you can't imagine a billion dollars, you'll never make a billion dollars. This takes us back to the idea of shifting your paradigm and manifesting what you want in your bank account.

I grew up in a family where I was introduced to meditation at the age of seven, learning Indian songs. My uncle used to bring a spiritual guide to our household, and I had to learn how to meditate correctly. It became a routine for us. But just because you're doing meditation, it doesn't mean you truly know how to meditate. In America, meditation has become a trend—everyone wants to go to meditation sessions, yoga, or Pilates. But often, people just follow the crowd, thinking like everyone else.

When you meditate, it's not about going to someone who does it every day as a job and just goes through the motions. If meditation is your job, you might be on automatic pilot, and you can't truly teach and pass on the skill. You can do it effectively if it's something you're passionate about, not something you do out of routine.

The key to meditation is deeply understanding its purpose. When you meditate, you switch paradigms—you shift from being awake to almost falling asleep, staying in that in-between state. That's when you switch your paradigm. The trick is to maintain that state, start asking questions, wishing for things, and imagining what you want regarding your health and feelings. It's about putting yourself in that state, manifesting from there, and working on it, almost like traveling within your mind.

It may sound complicated, but once you learn it, it becomes second nature. You can learn it in just a few sessions, and after that, you don't need anyone to guide you. The only reason we sometimes do meditation with others is that it's easier to have a guided meditation, where someone can lead you through the process.

When I do guided meditation, I guide people on what to think about—whether it's connecting with their inner child, focusing on the money they want to make, or staying on a specific thought. I guide them because many people can't guide themselves. They struggle to multitask when it comes to reorganizing their thoughts, especially when they're in that in-between state.

I've been to meditations in America where they say, "Don't think about anything, just relax," but that's completely wrong. The most connection you can have is when you meditate and manifest with intention. Manifestation isn't just something you do during meditation; you can manifest while you're awake. You can write down a goal, revisit it two years later, and see that you've manifested it.

There are so many ways to manifest, and I incorporate these into my meditation sessions and talks. Sometimes, I'll stop and encourage my audience to ask questions so I don't go too deep into certain topics. What I do with them is exactly what I do with myself every day.

Let's say you dress revealingly or sleep with a lot of men. This isn't the right way to go about things; you're just enslaving yourself to whatever it is. People tend to go on autopilot. When they don't have someone to give them feedback, to show them they're doing something wrong, putting themselves in danger, or not using their best potential, they're not going to know. Remember, we're stuck in our individual bodies, with one mind, and because we're in this physical form, we don't often have an outside perspective to truly see ourselves. It's super difficult for the average person to step out of their automatic mindset and observe themselves in the present moment. Most people just don't do that.

Because the majority of people don't self-reflect, it's hard for them to understand who they are and how the world perceives them. And that makes sense. How is this connected to spirituality? When you're self-absorbed, lacking self-restraint, and driven only by your urges—whether they're sexual, mental, or otherwise—how do you even know who you are? What are you afraid to confront? We're like computers, activated by external influences and people of interest. If we could just be honest and love ourselves, it would be all right.

But when someone has been through a lot, they need to correct their feelings and make sure they're not putting themselves in dangerous situations or engaging in excessive behaviors. On autopilot, though, they might not take responsibility or consider the consequences of their actions. It's about taking responsibility for the outcomes.

You don't have to be a saint, but you do need to have those inner conversations with yourself. For example, you might think, *I'm not going to go on this vacation to Mexico by myself because if I drink alcohol, I could get into trouble.* Or, *I'm not going to post overly sexy pictures online because I could attract predators.*

People need to understand that these internal inner conversations are crucial to our self-concept. You need to ask yourself these types of questions. I used to be on autopilot, just going through the motions. But now, looking back, I realize how important it is to understand each moment and truly be present.

So, live in the moment. When you're alone in the car, don't just let your mind wander aimlessly. When you go to bed at night, don't just shove your thoughts aside. Have that conversation with yourself. It takes time to develop this habit of self-conversation, but it's essential.

When you ask yourself these questions, you start to understand your actions and emotions. I'm not saying you have to overthink everything, but it's important to have an emotional connection to every decision you make. It's not just about the surface level; it's about understanding the substance behind your thoughts and actions.

Sexuality, like everything else in the world, needs to be understood on a deeper level. It's about understanding yourself and those around you.

I would never go to a debate unless I truly understood the topic and the facts behind it. Beyond the surface, I want to know what's really going on. You wouldn't put yourself out there to be used or abused if you were in tune with your innermost thoughts and feelings, with your mind, body, and actions connected as one. You'll be more sensitive to others because when you become spiritual, you understand something important. There's a saying in Hebrew that translates to, "When you cancel others, you cancel yourself." If you can't see others for who they are, you can't see yourself. When you learn to see others, you learn to see yourself.

That's why, when you cancel others, you're really trying to cancel parts of yourself that you don't know how to deal with. But when you reach a higher level of spirituality and understand yourself, you become more compassionate. You no longer see people as labels—the overweight lady, the ugly lady, the Black lady, the orphan, the Jew, or the Muslim. Instead of seeing the negative, your eyes may begin to choose to see things in a more positive light, like seeing the hardworking lady trying to lose weight rather than immediately judging others. Respect for others comes when you understand that we are not groups; we are individuals.

When you look at the Jewish religion, there are hundreds of thousands of types of Jews. The same goes for Muslims and Blacks—there are billions of people with diverse cultures, colors, and styles. No matter which group, race, or country an individual may come from, it means nothing. Your "label" does not define you. We are part of humanity, and you are the only one who can define your life. Many people practice religion without truly being a part of it—they do it out of fear of being judged by the people in their own religion or because it's all they've ever known. So, unfortunately, practicing their religion is being done on autopilot. Even if they want to change or disconnect, they feel trapped by society, family, and tradition. People are trapped in communities, countries, religions, and history.

But when you disconnect from all of that and focus on being yourself, you start to see the world differently. Even if you continue practicing your religion, practice being human first. For example, I could be from Israel, and there could be a conflict between Israel and Palestine. But when I meet Palestinians in America, I can meet amazing people who could be my allies. They might see things differently, perhaps because Israelis hurt their family, just as Palestinians might have hurt my family. Yet, in America, we can grow and see each other as humans.

The reason I talk so much about Palestinians and Israelis is that this subject has deeply affected me. As a human being, I constantly try to view the world as an outsider, like an alien observing us. When we see things this way, we no longer want to fight over land, religion, or possessions. I'm talking about both sides here. Is it really worth it to fight, bomb, slaughter, and rape over a piece of land that you believe belongs to you? Is it worth forcing your children to go to war for it? We are all human beings.

This world belongs to all of us who are born on this earth. We should love each other simply because we share the same existence as humanity. We are born, and in the end, we die. We don't have all the answers, and this is a painful reality for every human being on this planet. Every human being asks questions, and just as we share death, struggle, and obstacles as humanity, we should love and accept each other.

Even though I have my ideologies and see my religion in a certain way, even though I'm faithful to the place I come from—and I believe everyone should be faithful to their origins—I don't think Muslims, Jews, Christians, or anyone else should abandon their generational history, their family, and their ancestors. You should always be faithful first to your family, your people, your city, and your village. That's my point of view. But that being said, we should never forget to be human above all else. And if someone in your circle does something wrong, you should tell them, teach them, and open their eyes.

In my eyes, it's always about the spiritual world. The physical world is the hell that God wants us to face. And I'll tell you why. This world is completely physical. In the Gemara, one of the strongest books in the Torah, the physical world is called *Gashmi*. *Gashmi* means the world where you can touch, feel, smell, and taste. The *Gashmi* world tricks you—it's like drugs. It tricks you into thinking that you can do everything, that you're going to live forever and be young and beautiful forever. But before we came here, we were in a spiritual world, and after we leave here, we'll return to a spiritual world. This life is just a brief experience for our souls before we move on to the next level. It's a test to see how we behave in this physical *Gashmi* world.

When you study the Torah deeply, the biggest Kabbalistic rabbis isolate themselves from society. The biggest monks in Hinduism also isolate themselves. They do this because, when someone reaches a higher level of spirituality, they want to be alone. They can't bear to be around human beings because humans represent all the bad habits of humanity—all the *Gashmi* physical habits. We want to eat until we're sick, try everything, and explore everything. We always want more. Sexually, we have no boundaries; we want to experience everything because we think,

What the hell, let's abuse our bodies, let's try everything because I only live once. We want to spend all our money and buy all the clothes just because we can. But when you reach a higher level of spirituality, you no longer need all these possessions.

For example, Steve Jobs became disconnected from society because he reached a higher level of spirituality. I think he just didn't know how to translate it into spirituality because he was so locked into his agenda against religion. But I believe he understood a lot; he just didn't know how to bring it all together. This happens to many people in these confusing times. On the one hand, we want to be spiritual, but on the other, we're going against the natural spiritual paths that our bodies try to lead us on.

Judaism is a religion based on science. When Jesus walked on water and did all those miraculous things, it was because he was diving into Kabbalah and Gomorrah before the age of forty, which is forbidden. When you dive into these teachings as a man before age forty, you can do all these incredible things. That's why the Kabbalah says not to dive into it before you're forty because you can access super God-like powers. This is specifically what the Bible warns against—if you dive into it before you're forty, you tap into higher spirituality and God-level actions.

I read the Torah in Aramaic and Hebrew, and then in English, and because I talk to people all the time about religion, I've met with priests, rabbis, and Christians, and I even went to India to dive in and understand the outer and inner perspectives. A lot of religious leaders like priests, rabbis, and kadis have a mindset and belief so strong that it blinds their view completely. Because they have the title, the followers, the power, and are passionate about their beliefs, they end up indoctrinating people with such harsh judgment that they may send a person down the wrong path.

We aren't all made the same or meant to live the same lives. Even though we may be from the same religion, at the end of the day, we are individuals. Your life is your own, and it's up to you to decide what's best for you, personally. So, if you ever seek religious advice, remember that the world isn't black and white. We do not need to be zero percent or one hundred percent. All or nothing, take it or leave it. You do what's right for you, and you find your own middle ground.

But when you keep reading and learning more, you start to realize that this world is a simulation designed to deceive us and test how far we can go as humanity—as physical, biological beings—using and sometimes abusing each other. And then there's the light at the end of the tunnel. In the midst of all this, in the one hundred percent of humanity, you'll find that the majority of humans, less than one percent, are truly *humane*. That's why I sometimes play along with materialism—cars, women, clothes. I'm not going to be a hypocrite. I post photos on social media and engage with them because I'm a part of this physical *Gashmi* world. Even the Torah says that sometimes you have to play the game to not be out of the game. But as you play the game and become strong enough, you reach a point where you can give, teach, and contribute.

The Torah, Christianity, and even Islam—when you look at the real scriptures—all teach that you need to be giving, not taking. When you're constantly in a paradigm of taking, you're not going to achieve much spiritually. God, the universe, or whatever you may call it, might pour fame and fortune upon you, but the moment it decides to take it away, it will. You can have the best doctors taking care of your health, but if it's your time, it's your time. We cannot change that. Every human being needs to understand that if you don't get up in the morning with a sense of purpose—thinking about how you can help, give, and contribute—then you're lost.

Many people who get addicted to drugs, gambling, sex, or alcohol are just sensitive individuals who lack guidance and don't know how to manage their spirituality and feelings. If you don't know how to manage your spirituality and emotions, that's when you become completely lost.

This week, I was talking about balance with a business acquaintance who said, "Oh, I don't want to go there because the vibration isn't right for me; the feeling isn't right for me." But every time I'm around her, I sense vibes of jealousy, competition, impatience, and intolerance toward others' feelings. It made me realize that a lot of people, even good ones, struggle to translate their thoughts into action, to change their automatic responses from just talking to actually doing. If I had only witnessed her insensitive behavior toward others, I wouldn't think much of it because that's life, and there's always going to be shitty people you've got to tolerate. But the fact that she called out and looked down upon these negative behaviors and behaved in this exact manner made her a hypocrite. Hypocrisy is one of the worst things you can do if you're trying to elevate yourself. In fact, hypocrisy only brings you in the opposite direction: down. This is because behind hypocrisy lies denial, and anyone in denial will never be able to accept their flaws and grow from there.

And when I realized I was that kind of person a few years back, that's when everything went downhill. I lost everything—my health, my house, and my money. Why? Because I was just talking and not doing it. When you're just talking and not really connecting, not really taking accountability for not being patient with others, or not truly seeing others, it all falls apart.

I think back to when I was working with my mom at the salon about seventeen years ago. I'll never forget this lady who came in for the first time with her future daughter-in-law. She said the dress was too expensive, the whole deal was too much, and she couldn't go through with it. I didn't understand why it was such a big deal. Her daughter took me aside and explained that her dad had lost his job, so they had to watch every penny. I had a chip on my shoulder back then and didn't get it. I thought, *Okay, you lost your job, big deal, you can always get more money.* I actually said that. I can't believe that was me when I look back nearly twenty years later, but I said it. And then life brought me to that exact point—I didn't have a job, and I couldn't afford even a piece of bread and butter. Life taught me the same lesson I had dismissed in others. That's exactly what I mean by the simulation of life.

When I was twelve, I kicked a small dog because I was angry and because I had no control over my own life. I was being beaten badly at school, and then found I was finally bigger than something, so I kicked the dog—not severely. And later in life, I got that same kind of kickback, just in a different form. Because I'm super in tune with who I am and with the universe, every single thing I've done that wasn't aligned with my conscience comes back to me like a whisper in my ear. It sounds crazy, maybe even delusional, but I can trace them all back to their origins.

If you don't align yourself, if you don't teach yourself to be better, the universe will do it for you, whether you like it or not. And if you remain stubborn, refusing to learn from the lessons that keep coming, eventually, you'll expire—whether it's from an overdose, a heart attack, cancer, or whatever else the universe throws at you. The universe will give you many chances to work on yourself and to elevate yourself to a godly creature. And by "godly," I don't mean anything to do with religion but the highest version of yourself—your divine self.

That brings me to another Jewish book called *Kohelet* (Ecclesiastes). This book talks exactly about our behaviors and how they shape our lives. The behaviors we need to embody are often small yet significant. You should treat animals with the same care as you treat yourself, and treat other humans like they are your own family. If you see a guy begging for food outside a store, don't just say, "Ugh, he's homeless, forget him, I'm not going to help." Instead, buy him a sandwich. I'm not talking about those people on the street who clearly have money and are just panhandling as a job. We have the ability, the senses, the eyes to see, the mouth to speak, and the nose to smell and discern all these things. Everything that comes our way is an opportunity to become superhuman by being intuitive.

This intuition isn't just about how we interact with people on the streets but with the world in general. In every way, you have to contribute to yourself and not use and abuse yourself. This body isn't really ours, so we have no right to abuse it or overdo it. When I learned this, I stopped abusing my body by feeding it hate and started feeding it love. Do everything in moderation. Think about the outcome; think about the consequences.

Don't love anyone more than you love yourself. Don't hate anyone, either. Put that hate in a drawer and say, *Okay, I hate him, but it's in a drawer, and I'm not going to do anything with it.* We're all different. You might think of yourself as a superhuman, better than others, and that confidence can be beneficial to some extent, but in reality, you're not. At the end of the day, we all come from the same place and go into the same ground. It doesn't matter if you're rich or poor; they either burn you or bury you. Once we understand the game of this physical life, that's it.

Whatever you ask for is coming to you. I've manifested things. I can't talk about something huge that's happened yet, but I've manifested something big that I never believed I'd have the chance to even audition for. Things happen in the right way for our growth because if you want something too much and you're not ready for it, the universe usually won't give it to you. Look at all these Hollywood singers who started young, like Britney Spears. They weren't ready for fame, and without proper guidance, they got lost in the very things they wanted so much.

I've learned to accept reality as it is. For example, if I want someone so badly, but they don't want me, I put that feeling aside and say, *Okay, I accept reality. I'll go with God.* When you live in that mindset, let me tell you, you find so much more peace inside. Things happen in different ways, but they're stronger and better than what you expected.

I used to ask myself, six to ten years ago, *Why isn't my book happening? Why isn't it happening? Am I not lucky? Am I not good enough to publish a book? Am I not smart enough? Is it because I'm dyslexic, and everyone who ever labeled me as stupid was right all along?* That was my inner conversation. But why would you even want to write a book when you're thinking those things about yourself? Why would you want to give something to the world when you're in that mindset?

CHAPTER 10

First, personal growth involves a certain level of self-sacrifice. It's a misconception to think you can just go to a psychiatrist or psychologist, take care of yourself, and be fixed. You will never be completely fixed. There are choices I've made that I can never reverse. Second, I'm not living in a state of one hundred percent self-acceptance. I'm trying every day, but I believe self-acceptance is a journey. It's not something you achieve in one day and then declare that you accept yourself. It's an ongoing process because you constantly get reflections from the outside world.

For example, I'm very short (4'11"), so when I'm standing next to a tall woman, I don't really accept myself. Self-acceptance isn't some magic word or a self-help book that you read, and suddenly, you've helped yourself and now accept yourself. That's nonsense. If someone tells you that, they're lying. None of us, no matter how we look, even if we're the most gorgeous people, will accept it when we get older, when we're forty, fifty, or sixty. We age, and nobody fully accepts that.

I'm learning to have more tolerance for who I am. For example, I have scars on my hand. It is what it is; I can't make my hand look one hundred percent smooth again. I accept it, but I don't accept it in the sense of loving it or saying *I love my scars*. It's a different kind of acceptance. It's a more mature kind of acceptance. You accept the situation for what it is. Instinctively, we always aspire to perfection, even when it's impossible. It's just part of our nature.

It's like talking to a former porn star twenty years later—she may have accepted what she did, but she will never fully accept that it's her past and that she can never change it. It's a physical footprint, a digital footprint, a permanent footprint. We learn to have small levels of acceptance and to understand that, as adults, we can't make a big deal out of things we don't accept. We just accept them for what they are.

When you understand that, it becomes much easier to accept reality as it is. And when you accept reality as it is, that's the true acceptance. It's not about suddenly thinking you're perfect because you never will be. And anything that seems "perfect" isn't really perfect. We're always going to have doubts, and if something seems too good to be true, it probably isn't true. The only things that are truly big and accepted in the eyes of people are either God or whatever spiritual path they choose.

So, self-acceptance isn't about feeling like everything is perfect. It's different from that. It's about accepting the truth of who you are, where you are, and where you're at in life right now. It's just about accepting that truth.

Does this create a sense of freedom within you? For example, I know a lot of older women who are dating younger guys and telling themselves, *He fell in love with me; it's not about my money.* I've seen it so many times, and I think, *They may have a billion dollars, but they still haven't learned to accept reality.*

The more you accept reality, the less heartbreak you experience. Take this example: if you're in your sixties and dating someone in her twenties or thirties, it's important to be honest with yourself about why she's with you. If you convince yourself it's purely because of your personality or appearance, you're setting yourself up for disappointment. But if you stay grounded in reality and acknowledge the role that age, resources, or life stage might play in the dynamic, it'll hurt less if the relationship ends in your later years. Self-deception—whether about relationships or anything else—always leads to internal conflict. It creates a gap between what you know deep down and what you're pretending to believe. Over time, this can lead to secrecy, defensiveness, and misplaced anger. That's not a cycle you want to fall into.

It's better to always tell the truth, especially to yourself, because if you're not truthful with yourself, you can't be truthful with the world. I remember a time not long ago, just three years back, when I would wake up and find myself in five different Israeli Facebook groups, seeing posts about my character. People were saying, *"Do you know this woman, Sheena Reynolds? We're just trying to warn you about her. She's a scam artist who ran away from Florida. The FBI is looking for her."* All of this was a complete fabrication.

Because of these lies, people started canceling on me, scared to work with me based on what they read. I was left wondering, *What am I going to do?* Everywhere I went, people in my community thought I was a scam artist because this woman spread these lies. I had so many plans for my future and so much work I was doing. I was in Texas, working with people all day long, trying to build a life for myself, saving money to buy a house. But I was terrified. The lady I was working for knew a lot of Israelis. What if one of them told her that I was a scam artist or a bad person running from the law?

I was paranoid on a daily basis. The fear consumed me because I was in the middle of creating a new life. I thought, *If I become a top injector, if*

I get my name out there as one of the best because I change people's lives, then I'll make enough money to buy a house and do all the things I planned. But what if Americans found out about this embarrassment? I could tolerate the Israeli community gossiping, but what if it spread in America? What if people started believing I was a scam artist, a Mossad agent, or that I had killed people in Israel? Believe it or not, some people did believe that.

I was living in a state of paranoia almost every day, in fear of my fresh start being destroyed. My heart raced constantly, and I knew something had to change. I would wake up in the morning, do my breath work, drink a lot of water, go to the bathroom, brush my teeth, and then start my meditation. I always had that little voice in my head saying, *Focus on the end goal, focus on the end goal.* I told myself, *No matter what happens, don't get stressed when a problem arises. We'll deal with it when it comes.* I used to call myself by my name: *Sheena, don't forget, when the problem arrives, we'll deal with it.* Even now, when I sense a problem coming, I tell myself, *Wait until the problem really knocks at your door, and then we'll deal with it. Whenever it comes, we'll deal with it then.* There's no need to stress about something that might not even happen.

I reminded myself that America is more rational than Israel. I thought, *I'll show them the restraining order, the police evidence, and give them the number of the police sergeant. Just don't worry, everything's going to be okay.* I would nurse myself, talk to myself like a little girl, and comfort myself. It's a conversation I developed with myself: *Don't worry, everything's going to be okay. I'm always here for you.* Once, my son walked into the room and asked, "Mom, what are you doing? Are you talking to yourself?" And I had to make up an excuse, saying I was just thinking about something I was reading, so he didn't think I was crazy.

Then I realized that if I'm living in a constant cycle of fear because of this woman, that's like a psychological war. She's very smart, going to every single group on Facebook and making me famous by posting all my pictures from different eras of my life. She even wrote about my father being in jail and made up stories about me killing people in Israel. It was really psychological torture.

I had to raise my son through all of this, providing, saving, and driving from place to place. It was very difficult emotionally. But I always remembered one thing—you can truly change how you feel by listening to music. So, when I was feeling really down, I'd put on a song with lyrics like, "Don't let them fool ya, always rearrange ya, you got a life to live, don't go too hard." I'd sing it out loud and tell myself, *I'm winning, I'm winning, I'm winning.* I forced myself to only hear positivity, even when I was fighting with myself, thinking, *It's not going to help, so stop doing it. Nothing's going to happen. She's going to win; she's strong.*

In those moments when I felt like I was losing myself, I discovered that my willpower and my need to be successful were stronger than anything else. This need to overcome everything was stronger than anything else. I want to love myself. I want to give that little inner child in me a break, and I want to let her win and accomplish what she deserves.

But it wasn't just the stalker—it was the aftermath, the aftereffects of what happened to her. What followed was even worse than what she did. To explain, she was spreading all sorts of dangerous lies, and when your face is out there in a negative way, all the hateful people, all the jealous people, all the losers who can't accomplish anything, they see you working hard, running from place to place, being successful, and they start rising up, thinking of ways to bring you down.

A couple came to my house and said, "We want you to give us $40,000."

I was shocked and asked, "What? No."

They replied, "You better give it to us, and you don't want to find out what will happen to you and your son if you don't." I was confused, asking what they meant, and they said, "No, we're not playing games. This is exactly what we need." I had numerous people coming to me, trying to blackmail me, and asking for benefits or money. One girl came for Botox, and three months later, she asked for it again, claiming the Botox didn't work. I explained that it was three and a half months late, and it was not supposed to last that long. The instructions say it lasts between three to six months. She insisted, saying, "No, no, no, I'm going to sue you." And she really did. She took me to small claims court, and thank God, the judge told her it didn't last more than three months, so she lost the case.

But this put me in a vulnerable position, battling people I didn't know and didn't want to know. They would suggest things like, "Maybe you'll pass your house to me, and I'll do Airbnb," or "Maybe you'll do this, maybe you'll do that. I know your house is in California." I was firm, saying, "No, I'm not giving my house to anybody." But then they'd bring their men to try to convince me to give them my house.

So many things happened because of their lies and threats that it emotionally destroyed me so many times. I was really down and scared, wondering what was going to happen. Were they really going to take my house? Were they really going to do something I couldn't control? Did I have to give them $40,000? Did I have to give them $20,000?

Then, people started collaborating with her through Facebook. Three girls were working with her, writing things like, "Yeah, I know her. She did my Botox, but it didn't last, and she's a bitch. I sued her, and I don't know what she did with the judge. Does the judge think she's got connections?" It became so frustrating and exhausting.

I often thought, *What do I need to do?* If I gave up, it meant it would continue on social media. It meant that even if I went to Israel tomorrow, it would happen. Even if I went to Dubai, it would happen. It didn't matter where I went, it would happen.

All the stuff that came after what she did felt like the end of the world for me because I needed to prove myself. I was scared. I didn't know who to trust. Then, I dating this Israeli guy for three years, but it was a disaster. I was very sick, still working but fainting often, and he took me to the hospital. He was so sweet, and I was so happy. I thought, *He's not my usual type, but I need a man like this who takes care of me and helps me when I need him.*

Later, he told me that he initially thought I was a scam artist because of what she said. He thought I was doing cocaine and other things. He said, "When I started dating you, I was with you every day, and you were completely the opposite of what was written about you."

That's when I realized how much your character and reputation can influence people. When someone says bad things about you for so long, it starts to become the truth in others' minds. When you go through something like that, it's so easy to become angry and bitter.

How did I maintain my compassion? I would scream, "What just happened? This isn't fair. Life isn't fair." But then, I would remind myself that I needed to prove that I was stronger. When my mom or people in school told me I couldn't do something, that always triggered me to prove them wrong and do it even better. The more people tried to put me down, the harder I would fight against it.

Believe it or not, the goodness in a person always comes out. I have a lot of clients who tell me, "I didn't want to come to you. I've been thinking about it for a long time, but I was scared because people said you were involved with married men and other things." One woman told me her husband said, "There's no smoke without fire." I said, "I understand where they're coming from, but in my case, it's not true. I'm not a scammer. I didn't do anything to her. I don't even know her. She was never my friend or client. Yet, for eight years, she's been trashing me on social media. What can I do? It's one woman against one lunatic who has terrorized so many others, not just me."

But I've discovered the world will always find its way back into balance. One of the girls she was terrorizing in Israel sued her and won 200,000 shekels, and they're going to put a lien on her house. I'm proud of the girl for standing up for herself and succeeding. Eventually, the truth always comes out, and a price will always be paid. I'm sure my stalker's debt is nowhere near fulfilled, but that's not for me to worry about. Karma is running its course, and God is doing things the right way.

First of all, I really did take a lot of courses. I spent three years taking numerous courses on injections, specifically facial injections. Beyond that, I dove into learning about mortgages, including not just regular mortgages for houses but also those for RVs, land, and tiny houses. I covered the whole sector of making money through real estate, land, and RVs to understand my options as someone who didn't have much money to start with.

Then, I began to learn about finance, questioning why I had such a bad relationship with money. Why did I make money but always end up losing it? Why did I make money and never have any left in the bank? What actions was I taking that were causing this? It took me a few years to understand my relationship with money. I realized that money needs to be in constant flow. When you get money and see a large sum—say, $3,000 in two hours—it feels like a lot of money, especially if you're not used to having much. But you don't calculate that you won't make that much every day. If you only made $3,000 in one day and nothing else, it's just $3,000, not the huge windfall it might seem at first.

So, I had to adopt a new perspective with a different mindset about money. For example, I could make $3,000 in a day from injections, but only $150 from doing eyebrows. There was a period when I did three different things to earn that money, and in between, I learned how to better utilize my money.

When you study to become an injector, it's a riskier decision than deciding to become a doctor or a more secure profession because, as a doctor or nurse, everything is more straightforward. As an injector, you have to show all your course certificates, and then the health department comes to evaluate and decide whether to give you permission to work in that facility. But until then, you're the one investing a lot of time and money into your education to become an injector. A doctor has a guaranteed job, but I had to accept the fact that I would have to prove myself to every workplace I applied to and every client I took. There was a high chance of my putting in all those twelve years for nothing. Injectors are not saving lives compared to doctors, who can be of service to any living being. So, I almost blindly took that chance, with the future unknown. I studied psychology and majored in history until I decided on my new path. I had to take this seriously because this was my option. I wasn't going to be a doctor, so I decided to take this chance.

The first job I got as an injector started bringing in tons of money. When I say tons, I mean like $9,000 a week after deductions and the fifty-

fifty split. Then, I realized I needed to understand what to do with this money. When you've been really poor and had to count every penny for food and other essentials, suddenly having money makes you want to compensate yourself with things like clothes. I'm not a big spender by nature, but people would tell me, "You wear the same clothes all the time," or "It looks like you washed that too many times." So, I started buying clothes, flying to Israel, and I purchased the bed and the good mattress I always wanted.

I was focusing on the little things. But then, one day, I realized I was spending a lot of money. I paid off my debts, which was the most important thing to me because I knew that if I didn't deal with the debt, it was always going to hold me back. It didn't matter how much I made; the debt was always there. So, I had to pay it off. So, I started playing with the money, and I realized it was amazing. In this case, play meant divide and conquer. For example, let's say I made $10,000. I would put some money in my bank, some money aside for things I wanted, and some money for a food budget. I basically budgeted every single dollar that came in, and I realized that the people around me, who were working on salaries, didn't budget. They would see that when we would go out, I'd say, "No, I can't spend that much money. I'm not drinking alcohol, but I can't spend this." And they'd sit back and judge me for finally making money and choosing to spend it wisely, or in their words, "be cheap."

I realized they didn't budget; they just lived in the moment. This was particularly true in the middle class, who spend the most. They'd buy all the toys and think, *Oh, it's just payments.* But I realized I don't want anything to do with payments. For me, payments are a curse. I will avoid them at all costs because they mean something isn't fully mine, and I always have, and always will, hate the idea of owing something to someone. So, I learned how to budget and avoid the burden of owing money. To this day, I've made it this far without owning a single credit card. Just a debit card and that's it.

The financial system doesn't want you to be out of debt because then they're out of business. I started absorbing things differently, and I appreciated the gift of being able to see it from an outside perspective and break the twisted system they've created. Finally, I wasn't in the loop that I saw others get stuck in, completely controlling their lives and bringing them down. Just because everyone else is doing it does not make it automatically good. Everything regarding money was finally seen in a different light.

I also began to view relationships differently. For example, I saw men who worked all their lives and made money the hard way, and I thought, *Who am I to feel entitled to this guy's money?* I saw a lot of girls just looking for a man with money, and I wondered, *Why am I entitled to his money if he's been working hard all his life, just because I look good or whatever I bring?* I started to be more compassionate toward human beings, understanding how hard they work for their money.

When you start changing your perspective and observing the world and people in that way, things change in your life, too. I began to appreciate the little things. For example, from cleaning, I might make $200 a day; from doing eyebrows, I'd make $30 per person; and from fillers for lips, I'd make $450. Then I said, *You know what? I'm not discriminating against any income. Money is money. Whether it's a thousand dollars, four hundred dollars, or twenty dollars, it's the same—it's money that comes to the table.*

When I started having appreciation for the little money, I think that's when I started to receive the bigger money.

The little things matter, even the little lies, so breaking the habit of lying to yourself about even the little things makes all the difference. Anything dishonest will only harm you in the long run, including dishonest and negative relationships. This could be with your parents, your siblings, a man you love, a husband, or a girlfriend who's been jealous of you. You cannot have someone in your life who carries even an ounce of poison toward you. For example, if you have a friend who is always jealous or always has something negative to say—it's toxic. People don't necessarily have to see our vision or agree with us on everything, but I don't want to hear remarks like, "It's impossible, you could never make it," or "Come on, you're living in a dream, this is delusional."

You can't have that kind of negativity because, ultimately, deep down, we know exactly what's right and wrong if we follow our instincts. It's like stealing—you don't need someone to tell you not to steal. Deep down, it's not right. So, remove everything and everyone that drags you down energetically, physically, or emotionally. Bad relationships hold you back. Remember, the best and most important relationship is the one you have with yourself. When we repair this, it becomes way easier to enter and maintain healthy relationships.

If you don't love and respect yourself, if you don't listen to your body and your needs, no relationship can fulfill you. I see women and men working hard all day, trying to satisfy their spouses, boyfriends, or girlfriends. And if they don't succeed, they get upset. So, they keep working harder. When you remove these types of relationships from your life, it becomes easier to start building something better.

Correct your relationship with money. Don't be afraid of it. Don't be that pretentious person who thinks, *Oh, I don't love money. I don't care about money. Money is dirty; money is bad.* It's not. Money is the tool we have on planet Earth to move this materialistic world forward. You can't approach it with hatred or negativity, thinking it's inherently bad. It's really important to understand that you need to be surrounded by good energy. You don't have to be with people who tell you you're amazing or perfect every day, but you cannot be around people who secretly resent you, are miserable, or are jealous because that energy will destroy you.

I strongly believe in the power of energy—not in a primitive way, but in the sense that when someone sits next to you long enough, thinking, *She is so incredibly stupid, ha! I guarantee she will never see success.* Those thoughts and energy can take over the room, transferring to others whether they like it or not, almost as if these negative thoughts are breaking and entering into the surrounding people's minds and manifesting into reality. We have the ability to manifest, and when we look at other people in certain ways, we can manifest negativity for them without even knowing it. This is why we should tread cautiously with the thoughts we surround ourselves with, whether that be our company's or our own. Good energy is a gift, and we must treasure it.

I always made sure I dressed well, with makeup on and looking good, even when I was just at home. I looked top-notch. But the car I was driving was terrible—making noises, smoke coming out of it, and it looked like something straight out of a comedy movie. I had beautiful shoes, looked amazing, and I appeared all put together. Then, I would drive to the Four Seasons hotel, and the car would start making noise before they could even see it. The car started to make a lot of loud sounds a few minutes before I arrived. I remember pulling up and seeing all these millionaires and billionaires at the Four Seasons in Miami, and they were looking at me, driving this ridiculous car that didn't match how I looked. It was embarrassing. I had no place to park it because I had to bring suitcases and everything, so I had to bring my car. I couldn't afford to take Ubers everywhere. It was crazy. Completely, completely crazy. I knew I had to do something about it.

I had many embarrassing moments with cars and with the buildings I lived in. I didn't want a date to pick me up from certain buildings because I was embarrassed. People judge you, especially when you're dating with the intention of having a serious relationship, not just looking for someone to have dinner with. So, I decided not to date. My friends would ask, "How come you stopped dating?"

And I'd say, "Listen, I'm not where I want to be. I'm hustling all day long, working my ass off, driving this shitty car. I have to drive here and there. The jobs I'm taking are terrible. I'm studying. I'm definitely not going to date anyone right now."

Every time I went on a date, given the way I looked, they immediately assumed I was a gold digger or looking for a sugar daddy. But in the end, if I date someone for three, four, or six months, not being available at any time doesn't mean I am uninterested. It just means I am working to support myself and my son. You want to be able to go to your boyfriend and just tell him a story, not because you need something from him. You don't want to be in a position where you need something from someone, especially not a guy you like. I wanted to be in a real, sincere relationship where I could love my boyfriend, and he could love me to the extent that I felt free to say, "You don't understand what happened at work," without worrying that he'd feel superior or that I'd end up feeling like the relationship was about taking rather than giving and contributing.

So, I stopped dating for many years. I was all by myself, and my friends would ask, "How come you don't have sex? You don't have somebody you're seeing, like a friend with benefits?" I thought about that, too. But I'm an emotional person—I cannot sleep with someone and then go home, or have him go home, and feel like it was just sex, nothing else. I cannot separate the two in my head; I have a problem with that. I need to have feelings for the person I'm sleeping with, and that became an issue.

But in the end, it was for the best because I stopped dating. I didn't want to have more sex that would distract me or make me feel bad for having sex without love. So, I used that time to focus and create something out of nothing.

I became who I wanted to be.

I walked blindly, searching for that person I wasn't even sure existed, and I found her.

CONCLUSION

Even though your love life might be tough, or you might be in a great financial situation but not speaking with your family, or facing a business problem, it's easy to give up and get depressed. That's the natural response of the body to such situations. But it's much harder to sit down and lift yourself up. If you don't do it for yourself—if you don't motivate and support yourself—no one else will. And if they do, it's usually because they need or want something from you. It's rare to find people who genuinely help without any self-interest. I know some might think, *Oh, she's just saying this because she didn't have a close family,* but even if you have the best family, you still have to be the one to motivate yourself and be there for yourself. Life changes every few years—we lose people, and the world evolves—so it's crucial to continuously correct your inner dialogue and relationships. Remember, it's not something you start and finish; it's ongoing until the end of your life.

I've realized that people who claim to be my friends and offer help usually do so only when it's convenient for them or when it doesn't threaten them. They'll always choose what benefits them. Especially those who want to stay in your life—they may keep you around because you're connected to certain groups or people they want to be part of. You can't just cut off every relationship, but you must be aware that some people might jeopardize your success with a smile on their face, saying, "I love you; I'll always be there for you." They may do this as a way of keeping you close, but it's important to recognize the signs.

Never be afraid to push to maneuver things in your favor, not in a malicious way, but if someone is holding you back or doesn't want you to succeed, you need to be aware of that. It's crucial to always be mindful of the little signs, those small conversations, and cues. It may sound exhausting to always be vigilant, but if you want to succeed in business or as an entrepreneur, you'll encounter these challenges. If you prefer a simple life, just staying home with your family, then you don't have to worry about these things. But if you have bigger goals and want to achieve something significant, you must decide where you want to take your life.

If you want to be in business, especially as an entrepreneur, you'll be swimming with sharks in the big ocean. Your hands will get dirty, and you'll need strategies, end games, and the ability to foresee scenarios. You have to step up, learn the game, and be prepared. If you're not ready for that, it's better not to get involved because you'll only end up disappointed, perhaps even with yourself, if you don't have the willpower to succeed.

I never thought I would accomplish writing my book, especially not in English, and it's amazing. I ask that you don't prejudge me because I'm from Israel. Remember, no one chooses where they're born. I want you to see me as a human being, and I'll see you the same way. I'll judge you based on your actions and our interactions, not where you come from. And remember, don't judge anyone, including me. When we judge, we miss the opportunity to connect with someone who could change our life for the better.

Thank you so much for buying and reading my book. If you enjoyed it, I'd love you to share your experience, because that's what it's all about.

Let's Connect

Website: www.sheenarayreynolds.com

   Real_sheena_reynolds

   www.facebook.com/shina.ray.7

   @shina_reynolds

   @Ray_shina

www.ingramcontent.com/pod-product-compliance
Lightning Source LLC
Chambersburg PA
CBHW050257010526
44107CB00033B/1406/J